KAIT FENNELL

251

Things TO DO IN

ToFino

IT'S NOT
JUST ABOUT
SURFING

251 Things to Do in Tofino, BC

It's Not Just About Surfing

Updated Edition printed 2016

ISBN: 978-1537494807

Written By Kait Fennell

Book Cover Design & Layout by Joe Praveen Sequeira
Author's Photo, Credit Mélina Lamoureux

Acknowledgments

Many thanks for the insight, support and assistance of everyone who has contributed to the making of this book.

I'd like to thank my friends and family, especially my parents for their continuous love and support, my sisters, and the beautiful community of Tofino including the local Nuu-Cha-Nulth First Nations for sharing their traditional territory.

I'd like to also especially thank Tofino Mayor, Josie Osborne for sharing what Tofino means to her and for being the wonderful community leader that she is.

Sincere gratitude and thanks to the contributing authors of this awesome community, as listed: Agata Pydzinska, Alan Churchill, Johanna (Anna) Vanderkley, Anna MacKenzie-Sasges, Andy Herridge, Ariel Weiser Novak, Bree Eddy, Brendan Muehlenberg, Cameron Dennison, Camilla Thorogood, Caroline Woodward, Catherine Bruhwiler, Cedar James, Cindy Hutchison, Crazy Ron, Daniel (Daan) Delen, Dan Harrison, Dan Lewis, Danby

White, Daniel Lamarche, D'Arcy Boulton, Deborah McCartney, Andreane (Dede) Monette, Dom Domic, Donald Travers, Douglas Boulton, Drew Burke, Eugene Tom, George Patterson, George Smith, George Yearsley, Gisele Maria Martin, Glen Kaleka, Godfrey Stephens, Gord Austin, Hanna Scott, Ivan Gullic, Jaesn Singer, Jaime Ivars Hewitt, Jan Janzen, Janice Wong, Jean-Paul Froment, Jeffrey Beattie, Jerry Cloutier, Jesse Blake, Jessica Taylor, Jill Patterson, Joe Martin, John Wynne, Josh Temple, Kate Crosby, Kate Sitka, Kati Martini, Kayla McCloy, Kevin Midgley, Krissy Montgomery, Laurie Boudreault, Leah Austin, Liam McNeil, Lilly Woodbury, Lisa Ahier, Lisa Fletcher, Lise Saurette-Wynne, Lutz Zilliken, Marcel Zobel, Marco Procopio, Marcy Young, Mark Hobson, Markus Pukonen, Max Plaxton, Michelle Hall, Monte Clarke, Morgan Callison, Nate Laverty, Nicole Botting, Nicole Lohse, Ocean Simone Shine, Pascale Froment, Philipp Reimers, Rhonda Graham, Ryan Stewart, Samantha Hackett, Shandy Kariatsumari, Shawna Roberts, Sheila Orchiston, Sophie Laboissonniere, Sophie L'Homme, Stephen Dennis, Tamo Campos, Tanya Berger, Tanya Dowdall, Team Pacific Surf School, Thérèse Bouchard, Trina Mattson, Trish Dixon, Victoria Ashley, Warren Rudd.

Last but not least, I am truly indebted to **Joe Praveen Sequeira** for believing in me, helping and supporting me, making my dream a reality and getting me published. Thank you again.

Table of Contents

Visit www.251thingstodo.com/tofinoevents for updated annual events in Tofino.

Foreword

Growing up on Vancouver Island, Tofino was always a magical place for me to visit. There were childhood stays in the cabins at Pacific Sands Beach Resort, family camping trips to Green Point as a teenager, and university field trips in my 20s. I never imagined I'd be so lucky as to start my career as a fisheries biologist in Clayoquot Sound, but that's exactly what happened. I moved to Tofino in 1998 to work for the Nuu-chah-nulth Tribal Council, although for my first six years here I could hardly say I "lived" in Tofino. Instead of spending my days in an office, I was almost always out on the water or in a Nuu-chah-nulth community learning about herring, salmon, sea otters, clams, and all the myriad species that sustain the diets and culture of the Nuu-chah-nulth people.

One of the most important teachings I received in these first years in Clayoquot Sound was how profound the connection is between people and place and that this deep sense of connection can be found and fostered in the simplest of experiences. My career transitioned to the world of environmental education, where I had the privilege of taking small and large groups of children, youth, and adults to the forest, beach, and mudflats. Whether we discussed the relationship between fungus and tree roots, how barnacles feed, or why Western Red Cedar is also called the "Tree of Life," the highlight of these interpretive walks was always the moment when a person's face suddenly lit up, their eyes widened, and they uttered the magic words "Ah ha!" Invariably, the "ah ha" moment is a sudden realization of connection between people and place. One of my most memorable experiences as a naturalist was on the mudflats with a woman from New York City who'd previously had no idea that the white crust on the rocks at her feet were actually tiny living creatures (barnacles). As she suddenly realized that the intertidal zone was rich, complex, and full of life, she exclaimed that she would never forget this moment and that she would go home with a new way of looking at any beach she visited and what her impact on it might be.

Today, as mayor of this amazing community, I couldn't ask for anything more for a visitor to Tofino and Clayoquot Sound than to return home with a new way of looking at their personal connection to the world around us. This book is filled with tips and ideas of what to do during your time in Tofino, and it's chock full of insider insights from locals who have lived here for years. While you're here, strike up a conversation with a local, take the time to get to know us a little bit, and learn why we are all so passionate about this incredible, beautiful place we live in. Ponder your connection to these lands and waters, and take home some of the spirit of Clayoquot Sound so you can look out into your own world at home with new eyes.

-Josie Osborne
Mayor of Tofino

My Story

Hi, I'm Kait Fennell. You're probably wondering how I came up with this idea of *251 Things to Do in Tofino*?

I'm an obsessive surfer who has lived in Tofino for the past four years. I've been working in the service tourism sector; which helped me have free time to surf and travel. Since becoming a resident of Tofino, I've met hundreds, perhaps thousands, of visitors. Most of them have asked me many questions regarding Tofino, mostly the same type of questions, such as: what to do, where to surf, how to get to Meares.

Being in tune with people, I began to realize that many seemed completely lost when they arrive in Tofino! This is what gave me the idea of the book. I brought this up with my friend Joe Praveen Sequeira, and he said this is brilliant let's do it! And so this idea was born. I've put in a lot of time and effort into this as I know it will prove a valuable resource for future visitors coming into Tofino.

Well we did it! Welcome to Tofino! Come see from my eyes as a tourist turned resident and the eyes of many locals.

I hope you enjoy Tofino as much as I do and enjoy this book.

Learning More About
TOFINO
in Tla-o-qui-aht Territory

Head way west, you'll stumble upon the great Pacific Ocean and a little quaint town called Tofino. Ancient temperate rainforest stands strongly against the rich powerful ocean combining forces to create an explosion of life, where proud indigenous cultures thrive, and your adventure awaits!

Tofino in Tla-o-qui-aht (pronounced klaw-oh-kwee-awt "It's like a bear claw. The end sounds like getting a fishbone out of your throat." Joe Martin – Master Carver) traditional territory has a population of about 2000 year round residents. This number does not include the surrounding First Nations communities of the Hesquiaht, Ahousaht and Tla-o-qui-aht Nations. During the summer months, this population swells upwards to 20,000 including seasonal workers and visitors.

Tofino is located on the tip of the Esowista Peninsula, on the west coast of Vancouver Island, in British Columbia, Canada. It is at the southern edge of notable Clayoquot Sound, designated a UNESCO Biosphere Reserve. With one side facing the beautiful sound and inlet waters, the other side faces the wild open great Pacific Ocean.

Tofino is the official western terminus of the TransCanada Highway thereby designating it as the "End of the Road" or as some like to call it, including many local First Nations people, the "Beginning of the Largest Ancient Highway", the Pacific Ocean.

Every year, over 20,000 gray whales migrate past Tofino on their way north. Thousands upon thousands of migrating shorebirds come to rest and feed as well on the pristine mudflats of Clayoquot Sound.

Tofino is absolutely soaked in history. It begins 200 million years ago, more or less. But here are some more recent highlights.

Inhabited for many thousands of years by the Tla-o-qui-aht Nation people, Tofino is nestled in traditional Tla-o-qui-aht Territory.

The original native name for Tofino is Naachaks. It means "lookout". Much later, European settlers named it after the nearby Tofino Inlet in 1909. Tofino Inlet was named in 1792 by Spanish commanders, in honour of their admiral.

The ***first trading post and hotel*** was established on Stubbs Island around **1875** where traders came from all over the world to exploit the much sought after sea otter pelts which were sold to European markets and China, driving the sea otter population to near extinction. No sea otters = more sea urchins = disappearing kelp forests, which are crucial for the survival of many species. With a ban on sea otter hunting in BC, their numbers are finally returning, and you can spot these cute furry critters all over Clayoquot Sound.

The **Second World War** had a huge impact on community development, with the establishment of an air-force base.

Tofino and the surrounding communities were only accessible by boat until 1959. After, a road was finally built through the mountain pass which successfully connected Tofino to the rest of Vancouver Island. This road was paved in 1972.

With the **70's** came the huge herring *fisheries boom*. Fishermen, migrant workers came flocking to get their chunk of the pie. Money was flowing. Supposedly a kid could make $20,000 in a single night! Briefcases with gold bars handcuffed to their arms...absolute craziness. The whole town reeked of herring and money. Boom and bust.

Pacific Rim National Park was established in **1970** by Parks Canada. The Hippies have arrived to Wreck Bay! (now known as Florencia Bay). The old Wickaninnish on Long Beach was party central. Former prime minister of Canada, Pierre Trudeau, father of current prime minister, Justin Trudeau, surfed Long Beach for the first time.

Large scale logging operations in the area in the 1980s and 1990s meant a few jobs, but much conflict.

From 1980-1994, opposition to logging in Clayoquot Sound was expressed in several peaceful protests and blockades of logging roads initiated by the Tla-o-qui-aht First Nations.

Meares Island was formally declared a *Tribal Park* in **1984** by the Tla-o-qui-aht First Nations.

In **1993**, the largest act of civil disobedience in Canadian history happened right here! Over 800 protestors, including grandmothers, were arrested for standing up and protecting Clayoquot Sound from logging. Protectors included local residents, the Tla-o-qui-aht First Nation, Ahousaht First Nation, and environmental groups such as Friends of the Clayoquot Sound.

In **2000**, *Clayoquot Sound* was designated a *UNESCO Biosphere Reserve*. en.unesco.org

In **2007**, Tla-o-qui-aht First Nations pushed ahead to instill traditional teaching principles, by signing an agreement with the District of Tofino to pursue joint sustainability, and partnering with Parks Canada on a Tribal Parks Establishment Project, with the main focus on Haa'uukmin (Kennedy Lake watershed).

In **Spring 2015**, the Tribal Parks was officially expanded to all of the traditional territories of Tla-o-qui-aht which includes *Tofino*. A first in Canadian history.

To learn more about the history of Tofino, I recommend reading the book *"Tofino and Clayoquot Sound: A History"* by Margaret Horsfeld and Ian Kennedy. Also, *"Long Beach Wild"* by Adrienne Mason, or if you ever have the special opportunity, listen to an elder of a Nuu-chah-nulth Nation.

Climate in Tofino

Tofino has a very temperate climate.
Warm winters (warmer than both
Victoria and Vancouver) but cool
summers. As long as you have a nice
warm cozy wool sweater, rain coat,
warm boots, and a toque (Canadian
slang for a warm knit cap) you'll be the
happiest camper in Tofino. These are
crucial year round Tofino fashion items.

It's so temperate and mild here year
round, certain locals grow exotic palm trees in their backyard!

Sometimes, we are lucky to have one day of snowfall per year,
melting within a few hours, making it the least snowy place
in Canada. It rains roughly 200 days out of the year which
provides for our beautiful beloved temperate rainforest. I
personally, along with many other locals, absolutely love the rain!
Embracing the rain is a crucial element in living here.

In the winter months, large powerful storms frequently pass,
bringing lots of rain to feed our temperate rainforest.

Similar to the rest of BC, summer may sometimes bring drought
like conditions, hence water shortages. The grass may turn
yellow, rivers dry, mainly because of the differential heating
patterns of the ocean and land. A lingering area of high pressure
is created when the sun heats the land much faster than the
ocean. However, we do receive much more rain in summer
compared to the interior of BC.

Tofino Random Facts, *Local Stories* + *Gibberish*

Don't Mess With Orcas!

Many people think the great white shark is the top predator of the ocean, but this is a myth. The Orca also known as the killer whale is the dominant predator and has also on many documented occasions been known to hunt great whites for their fatty livers. They are highly intelligent social beings that analyze and develop individual hunting strategies to kill any kind of prey. Strategies can take years to perfect and then it is passed from one generation to the next. The orcas have three different cultures off our coast:

Resident Killer Whales...	**The Transients...**	**Offshore Type Killer Whales**
found on the BC coast, Washington and Alaska, which are fish eaters and travel in large groups remaining very local.	*tend to have a larger range. They live in smaller groups and specialize in eating mammals.*	*travel in very large groups, are the most vocal, and eat fish. Groups can reach a hundred.*

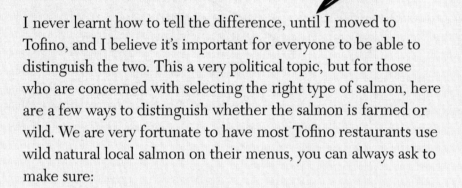

What The Heck Is the
Difference Between
Wild & Farmed Salmon?

I never learnt how to tell the difference, until I moved to Tofino, and I believe it's important for everyone to be able to distinguish the two. This a very political topic, but for those who are concerned with selecting the right type of salmon, here are a few ways to distinguish whether the salmon is farmed or wild. We are very fortunate to have most Tofino restaurants use wild natural local salmon on their menus, you can always ask to make sure:

»» Wild salmon usually has a darker deeper red color to it. Lighter pink/gray looking salmon are usually from fish farms.

»» You'll notice larger fatty white lines in the loin section of the fish. Wild salmon has firmer and leaner flesh. This is the difference between the quarterback and the couch potato.

»» There are no commercially viable Atlantic salmon fisheries left in the world. So if it's Atlantic Salmon, it's farmed.

Why "Tuff City"?

You'll most likely see and hear the name Tuff City around town. It originated during the herring fishing season, years ago. "This place was crazy with fish, herring all over the bay! Hundreds of boats everywhere! The whole harbor looked like a city. All of these fishermen would come up the hill and gather at the old Maquinna Pub. Suddenly, someone would start a fight and the whole bar room would burst into a brawl. A lady would walk in, and all these men would be fighting over her. And that's how Tofino got its name. You got to be tough to go to Tough City." Joe Martin – Master Carver

What is a **Tribal Park?**

Tofino is home to the very first Tribal Parks in North America, a movement that is growing across the nation thanks to the Tla-o-qui-aht First Nation.

The main challenge we face in areas like Clayoquot Sound, is balancing conservation and sustainability with human activity. Keeping the wild in wild, and our distance/impact from surrounding pristine areas. Clayoquot Sound is a sanctuary to many species. Tribal Parks is an integral part of this solution!

"The Tribal Parks system to me is very important. In the beginning it was only Meares Island Tribal Park but now it has expanded to all the traditional territories of Tla-o-qui-aht, which includes Tofino. I'm really happy that Tofino accepts this declaration from our people. Now, in order to be welcomed here, people need to acknowledge to always be respectful of our laws which pertain to nature. We all have to live here, so we all have to pull up our socks so to speak."

Joe Martin, Master Carver, Tla-o-qui-aht Nation.

What is the difference between a **park (Pacific Rim)** and a **"tribal park"?**

According to the Tribal Parks website, "A park is usually a protected area which excludes most human activities apart from recreation. A tribal park integrates human activities while caring for the ecosystem at the same time – this was done successfully by our ancestors, resulting in superior ecological integrity of the whole landscape in the territory."

There are now four Tla-o-qui-aht Tribal Parks, encompassing the entire Tla-o-qui-aht traditional territory:

⬆ **Wah-nuh-jus – Hilth-hoo-is (Meares Island)**

⬆ **Ha`uukmin (Kennedy Lake Watershed)**

⬆ **Tranquil Tribal Park**

⬆ **Esowista Tribal Park**

How YOU can support the **Tribal Parks Initiative:**

Walk the legendary Big Tree Trail in Wah-nuh-jus – Hilth-hoo-is (Meares Island) Tribal Park.

Go for an adrenaline pumped zipline tour in Ha`uukmin (Kennedy Lake Watershed) Tribal Park.

These are just a few of the ways you can experience Tla-o-qui-aht Tribal Parks and support sustainable First Nations economic activity in Clayoquot Sound.

TO LEARN MORE: Feel free to drop by the Tla-o-qui-aht Administration Office beside the Best Western Tin Wis or call at 250-725-3350 Terry Dorward, www.tla-o-qui-aht.org

Why Does the **Sea Sparkle At Night?**

Glowing zooplankton. Most bioluminescent zooplankton do not glow in the dark themselves. Instead, they squirt globs of glowing chemicals into the water as a defense mechanism. So cool! Make sure to check out this magic by the seashore at night.

What Is This **Body Of Water I'm Looking At?** **What's An Inlet?**

Ahh the Tofino Inlet! Is it a lake? The ocean? A river?

An Inlet is often a long and narrow recess along a coast, such as a small bay or arm that often leads to an enclosed body of water, which in our case is a sound. It is the connection between a sound and the ocean and can be often called an "entrance". A sound is a complex of large inlets or fjords. Clayoquot Sound has many inlets and islands, with Tofino Inlet being one.

What Are Those Big Barges Anchored in The Tofino Inlet For?

About 95% of the large barges you see sitting in the middle of the inlet looking out towards Meares Island (Wah-nuh-jus) are for the transport of supplies to and from the numerous fish farms that dot Clayoquot Sound. The majority of the fish farms are owned and operated by a large Norwegian owned company called Cermaq.

Never ever feed or approach wild life. As soon as a predator becomes habituated with humans/pets, they lose their sense of fear, and that places them in extreme danger of having to be shot, and is also a danger for humans.

What **TO DO** *if you encounter a:*

Bear - Don't run. Pick up small children and stay in a group. Back away slowly and talk in a soft voice. Don't make direct eye contact. Leave the area or make a wide detour. The bear will almost always give many warnings to give him space before any potential attack. Attacks are very rare, and they are more afraid of you.

Wolf or Cougar - Don't run. Pick up small children and stay in a group. Make yourself look big and aggressive by waving your arms and shouting, these predators hate confrontation. Make and maintain direct eye contact, throw rocks/sticks if needed. Never turn your back. Back away slowly, creating space between you and the animal.

10 **Tips** *on How to Act Like a* **Local Tofitian**

01 Wear a flannel shirt, gumboots, and a toque. Just be comfortable! We don't ever dress up.

02 Carry a Tofino Brew Co. Growler with you or have a coffee in hand in either a re-usable mug or an actual glass/clay mug/mason jar.

03 Have a medium to large sized dog by your side.

04 Talk about the surf, the swell forecast, anywhere anytime. You don't even have to surf, just talk about it.

05 Ask when ordering/buying food: Is that Local? Wild? Organic?

06 Walk, bike, or skateboard to where you need to go.

07 Never say TOE-FINO, locals pronounce it as TUH-FINO or simply Tuff.

08 Always take your wetsuit off at the beach, unless it's freezing cold and you live nearby. NEVER grocery shop in your wetsuit.

09 Do not drag your surfboard/SUP leash anywhere anytime, this defines the word kook, someone with no understanding of the sartorial and social norms of surfing culture.

10 A headlamp is your best friend.

How to Talk Like a **Local While in Tofino**

☞ Ucluelet = Ukee
☞ That's cool = Rad! Sick! Awesome!
☞ Tofino = Tuff or Tuff City
☞ Wickaninnish = Wick
☞ See you later= Chuu!

Useful Items *to Have While You Are in* **Tofino**

☞ Gumboots/Rainboots
☞ Rain Jacket, Rain Pants
☞ Wetsuit
☞ Headlamp
☞ Binoculars
☞ Waterproof Camera/GoPro
☞ A copy of "**251** *Things to Do in Tofino*"

How to Get to **Tofino**

There are a number of ways to get to Tofino. Most likely you'll fly into Vancouver International Airport if you are coming from afar. There are connecting flights from Vancouver to Nanaimo Airport, Comox Valley Airport, Victoria Airport.

From Vancouver Airport, you can rent a car or take public transit (Vancouver public transit is great!) or taxi to one of the two ferries that take you to Vancouver Island.

☞ *www.maps.google.ca*
☞ *www.avancouvertaxi.com*
☞ *www.bcbudget.com*

Or you can opt to fly direct from Vancouver International Airport to Long Beach Airport (Tofino). This is a 45 minute flight which you can book through Orca Airways, or KD Air. There are also private charters with Tofino Air and Atleo Air direct from Vancouver or Nanaimo.

☞ *www.flyorcaair.com*
☞ *www.kdair.com*
☞ *www.tofinoair.ca*
☞ *www.atleoair.com*

If you choose the ferry from Vancouver: There's the Horseshoe Bay Ferry (the easiest) in North Vancouver and there's the Tsawwassen Ferry South Vancouver.

☞ Schedules listed here: *www.bcferries.com*

If you choose the Horseshoe Bay Ferry, it's a 2-hour boat ride, to Departure Bay, Nanaimo. Here you can rent a car (if you don't already have one), or take the Tofino Bus Service schedules here:

☞ The Tofino Bus takes 5 hours to Tofino and you can choose to be dropt off in Ucluelet, or Tofino (Cox Bay Info Center, Lynn Road, or in town). ***www.tofinobus.com***

☞ By car, it's roughly 3.5-4 hours to Tofino from Nanaimo.

From the Tsawwassen Ferry to Duke Point. This ferry takes 1.5 hours and you arrive just outside of Nanaimo. There are no Tofino buses from this ferry, so you'll most likely need to have a car. From here it's roughly a 3.5-hour drive to Tofino.

If you are coming from Victoria, it's approximately a 5-hour drive to Tofino. You can fly direct as well to Long Beach Airport with Orca Air or KD Air. Or take the Tofino Bus from Victoria to Tofino.

☞ ***www.tofinobus.com***

☞ ***www.flyorcaair.com***

☞ ***www.kdair.com***

The drive from Nanaimo to Tofino will take 3 hours but you should give yourself at least 5 hours. Be careful, drive slow, it's super narrow, windy with hairpin turns. Please use the designated pull-outs if there's traffic behind you. There's lots to see along the way such as:

- ☞ Cathedral Grove BC's Big Tree Heritage Site (15 minutes on Highway 4 outside of Nanaimo)
- ☞ Goats on the Roof in Combs
- ☞ The views from Kennedy Lake (which is so big, you'll probably mistaken it for the Pacific Ocean)
- ☞ Rest on the rocks at Kennedy River

Clayoquot

Getting Around **Tofino & Clayoquot Sound**

In the summer time, the town of Tofino can become super congested, parking is extremely difficult.It is much easier to leave your car at the hotel/B&B/resort/vacation rental and take advantage of our wonderful Multi Use Path (MUP) by biking, skating, running or walking.

It's roughly a 20-minute bike ride to Town from North Chesterman Beach, and a 35-minute walk.

If you absolutely must have your car, you can park it at the Live to Surf/ Beaches Plaza and rent a bike. Your body and mind will thank you!

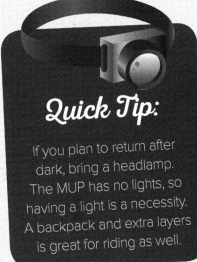

Quick Tip:

If you plan to return after dark, bring a headlamp. The MUP has no lights, so having a light is a necessity. A backpack and extra layers is great for riding as well.

We are very limited on taxis in Tofino, so please be mindful of that.

TOFINO TAXI:

250-725-3333 (Office)
250-266-2545 (Mobile)

Tofino Transit Shuttle FREE *(seasonal)*

Operates end of June-September. Runs hourly between 10:00 am and 8:30 pm. Another great transportation option and it's FREE!

This bus takes you to and from Tofino as far as Cox Bay Info Center. The bus has a few scheduled stops, but mostly you have to flag the bus driver to stop. Surfboards are welcome but NO BIKES.

For schedule visit: www.tofinobus.com/transit

Tofino Beach Bus

The Beach Bus operates daily, summer to mid-October from Tofino to Ucluelet with stops in the Pacific Rim National Park in between.

Surfboards and **Bikes** are both welcome!

Use the Beach Bus schedule to plan your adventure!

For fares and schedule: www.tofinobus.com/beachbus

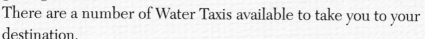

Water Taxis

Navigating around Clayoquot Sound can be intimidating. But getting out on the water, is a must! There are a number of Water Taxis available to take you to your destination.

If you are unfamiliar with the area, I'd highly recommend against taking your own watercraft, kayak, stand up paddle board without an experienced local. The waters can be very dangerous and complicated. We sometimes call the inlet the Tofino River because of the strong tidal currents flowing in and out.

Water Taxis Based in Tofino

Tofino Water Taxi/Poseidon's Adventure Center

On demand departures. Call Dispatch to make a reservation, then meet them on the dock at the end of Main St. across from the Hostel. *www.tofinowatertaxi.com* 1-866-794-2537 or 250-725-8844

Ocean Outfitters

Tofino Adventure Specialists. 368 Main St. *www.oceanoutfitters.bc.ca* 1-877-906-2326 or 250-725-2866

Jamie's Whaling Station

606 Campbell St. *www.jamies.com.* 1-800-667-9913

Remote Passages Marine Excursions

51 Wharf St. *www.remotepassages.com.* 1-800-666-9833 or 250-725-3330

Tofino Boating Co

Call Dan Currie for rates and fun! 250-266-2578

Water Taxis Based in Ahousaht

Eagle Adventures Water Taxi
Ed and Annie Smith, tours from Tofino to Ahousaht &
Hotsprings Cove, Whale Watching, Bear Watching.
250-670-9587 or cell: 250-720-6487

Cougar Island Water Taxi
Tours from Tofino to Ahousaht & Hotsprings Cove. Whale
Watching, Bear Watching, Sport Fishing.
250-670-9692

GI Charles Water Taxi
Tommy Stuart, services between Tofino, Hesquiaht (Hot
Springs Cove) and Ahousaht.
250-670-2456 or 250-731-7758

White Star Water Taxi
Peter Frank, services between Tofino,
Hesquiaht (Hot Springs Cove) and Ahousaht.
250-670-9683

Float Charter Planes

Atleo River Air Service
Proud to be the ONLY locally owned and
operated airline in Tofino. Full of local knowledge.
1-866-662-8536 *www.atleoair.com*

Tofino Air
Specializing in scenic flights and charter service for West
Coast Vancouver Island. Scheduled flights to Hot Springs
Cove and Ahousaht. 1-866-486-3247 *www.tofinoair.ca*

The Nuu-cha-nulth Nations

"What I truly love about Clayoquot Sound and Tofino is the interaction with the old timers and Nuu-Cha-Nulth people. Their humor is beyond; they can outdo anybody in the humor department (Ie: 'Godfrey your face is getting longer every day.' I asked 'What do you mean?' he said 'Well it goes all the way from your nose to the fringe of your bald head, an airport for mosquitoes!' I asked 'How come few Native people go bald?' he said 'You white guys think too much!') I love the native culture, the language, their humor, and the history!"
Godfrey Stephens, West Coast Artist

Humour is an intrinsic part of life in many First Nation communities. It's very important to laugh. Adding humor to story telling makes it that much better!

"Sometimes when we went over to listen to an Elder he would be talking and laughing and saying 'life we have to be serious but we also have to have fun, it's important also

to laugh' He would tell funny stories in our language and Dad and Mom would be laughing and I'd be sitting there and it would be only in our language, until I went to school then it was English and Latin together for the church."
Joe Martin, Master Carver and member of
the Tla-o-qui-aht First Nation

The Nuu-chah-nulth which means "all along the mountains and the sea" are composed of 14 different nations along the west coast of Vancouver Island.

Did you know: That the Nuu-chah-nulth coastal people have inhabited this area for an estimated 10,000 years or more! It is estimated that over 100,000 coastal people lived up and down the west coast!

Very important life rules for the local Nuu-chah-nulth are:
Iisaak = Living Respectfully
Qwa'aak qin teechmis = Life in the Balance
Hishuk ish ts'awalk = Everything is One and Interconnected

There are three main local First Nations around/within Clayoquot Sound:
1.   Tla-o-qui-aht Nation
2.   Ahousaht Nation
3.   Hesquiaht Nation (pronounced Hesh-kwit or Hes-kwee-at)

All of these coastal nations have always been deeply connected to the rich bountiful waters and temperate rainforests here on the west coast.

What used to be a nation of around 10,000 for the Tla-o-qui-aht remains at 900. Ahousaht Nation is the largest at a population of 2000. And Hesquiaht 650.

The villages of **Hesquiaht** (Hot Springs Cove, Hesquiaht Harbour) and **Ahousaht** (Marktosis and many others) are located north of Tofino and are boat and floatplane access only. For the experienced kayaker/paddler, you can reach these villages on Flores Island and Hesquiaht Harbour over a multiple-day adventure, permission needed prior from the from the Tla-o-qui-aht Administration Office 250-725-3350.

The **Tla-o-qui-aht village** of **Opitsaht** is visible directly across Tofino inlet. Located on Meares Island. The easiest way to remember the name, is to think "Opposite Tofino=Opitsaht". Another village called **Esowista** and **Ty-histanis** (an expansion of Esowista) is located on the north end of Long Beach.

Opitsaht is one of the longest continually inhabited villages on Vancouver Island, perhaps even in North America. If you head into the Whale Centre, you'll be awed by the number of ancient artifacts that have been discovered in the area and are still being discovered today, such as ancient spear heads, fish traps, etc.

Tofino and Clayoquot Sound are soaked in many amazing historical stories, you just need to look beyond the craziness of the colonization period where all history was shared through story telling, dances, songs and art.

If you are interested in learning the Nuu-cha-nulth language, www.nuuchahnulth.org/language/language.html is a great start!

251
Things TO DO IN

ToFino

Trails & Hikes

Trail lengths (km/mi) noted are the roundtrip distance. We are fortunate to have well maintained trails; many are an educational experience with readings along the way.

01 **Meares Island Big Tree Trail.** Getting there is part of the fun. Take a 10-minute water taxi boat ride, stand up paddle board, kayak or canoe to the island. Easy 1.2 km (0.75 mi) on boardwalk, and an optional moderate 3 km(1.86 mi) loop trail. Note: if you plan to rent a kayak/ SUP/canoe, have an experienced guide with you; the inlet has very strong currents and heavy traffic at times.

02 **Lone Cone Mountain.** Difficult 6.6 km(4.10 mi) trail for the avid hiker who likes a challenge. Take a 15-minute water taxi ride to the North-Western end of Meares Island to access the Lone Trail head. It's four to six-hour hike from pier to pier, and 15-20 minute boat ride to the trailhead. Best to hire a knowledgeable local guide. Obtain permission and directions to hike the trail from the Tla-o-qui-aht Administration Office 250-725-3350 or if you stay with Lone Cone Hostel & Campground on Meares Island, they'll arrange everything for you.

03 **Vargas Island Telegraph Trail.** Easy 7 km(4.35 mi). A big kayak destination, you can take a water taxi, canoe, SUP or kayak to this unique flat island. The trail takes you across the island to Ahous Bay where you may possibly spot some whales. There's no reliable water sources, so take lots of water, and there's a pit toilet at the south end of Ahous Bay. No trail fees. The lack of amenities arguably is a good thing because it keeps the natural beauty of the area intact.

04 **Wildside Heritage Trail.** Moderate 11 km(6.84 mi). This trail runs through a thick rainforest of ancient Sitka trees on Flores Island in Ahousaht Territory, passing Whitesands Beach and Cow Bay leading to Mount Flores. Open only May-October. There's a $25/person access fee for maintenance, which is payable at the trail office, online or to one of the authorized trail staff. For more information, visit: www.wildsidetrail.com

05 **North Chesterman Beach to Frank Island to South Chesterman Beach.** Walk from one to the other on low tide. Touch the far rocks at North Chesterman below the Wickaninnish Inn and head south!

06 **North Chesterman Beach to Cox Bay Beach.** If you are in Tofino around the time of the super tide it is possible to hike from North Chesterman all the way to Cox Bay on the extreme low. But make sure you time it right so you can still return the same way you came.

07 **Cox Bay.** Park at Malty Road on low tide, walk the path to the beach and head south to touch the big rock (the beginning of the Pacific Rim National Park), from here you can climb to Cox Bay Lookout or turn back around and head north on the dead low tide, walking length of Cox Bay continuing around the corner to Rosie Bay to the big rock before you hit South Chesterman. Explore the few rock caves here, and see if you can find some sea star friends and anemones.

08 *Sun down* **Radar Hill.** This hike is short and easy with stunning views, especially at sundown. A series of radar stations throughout Canada/US were built during the cold war in 1954. Before it was completed, it was obsolete, and today only the cement foundations remain. Back in the day, the town bought the building for a $1 and moved it to the lot next to Schooner Restaurant.

09 Pettinger Point. At the North end of Cox Bay, the entrance is at Pacific Sand Beach Resort. Hike along the boardwalk through the rainforest to the rocky point. Great view of Rosie Bay, and possibly you'll see some surfers.

10 Schooner Cove. Easy 2 km(1.24 mi), one of the best! If you are craving a little bit of isolation and want to escape the common beaches, hike down to Schooner Cove, one of the rarer desolate beaches around Tofino. You may be lucky to find a Japanese fishing float during your adventure. Get dropped off by the Tofino Beach Bus and walk the entire length to Long Beach.

11 Long Beach. Want a real challenge while maximizing cardio? Hike the whole length of Long Beach for real. The length of Long Beach, Comber Beach and Wickaninnish Beach is 12 km(7.46 mi)…not far enough for you? You can even cross beaches at low tide if you time it properly.

12 **Combers Trail/ Spruce Fringe.** Easy 4 km(2.49 mi). At the edge of Long Beach, this trail starts as gravel then becomes a boardwalk leading to a very thick dense forest closer to the sea where the trees contort and huddle together to protect themselves from the weather.

13 **Rainforest Trail.** Easy 1 km(0.62 mi) loops. Walk along boardwalks through the ancient green forest where you will see beautiful towering ancient cedars. Choose to do one loop or both. Perfect for a rainy day, since the tree tops provide a natural canopy, as you learn about the ecology of the rainforest from the educational signs along the trail.

14 **Shorepine Bog Trail.** Easy 0.8 km(0.50 mi). This is a very unique trail. Due to a poorly drained ecosystem, we have this beautiful bog with ancient trees. Learn why the trees are stunted and gnarled in this unique area.

15 **Nuu-chah-nulth Trail.** Easy 2.5 km(1.55 mi). It starts behind the Kwisitis Visitor Centre on Wickaninnish Beach. A section of the boardwalk turns into a preserved area of original plank wood that pioneers placed to travel between Ucluelet and Long Beach. Study the plants closely as the forest changes from bog, stunted trees and berries, to mossy green rainforest with large cedars. After rain, may be muddy.

16 **South Beach Trail.** Easy 1.6 km(0.99 mi). Start at the Kwisitis Visitor Center heading south to South Beach, one of the top beaches on the West Coast for storm watching. Massive waves roll through during the winter due to the funneling action of the headlands. Walk along the coastline on a well-maintained, level boardwalk/pathway. You'll pass a totem pole and many small beaches along the way.

17 **Willowbrae Trail.** Easy 3.4 km(2.11 mi). A nice quiet trail, this is part of the old route that the earliest settlers and First Nations took to get from the head of Ucluth Inlet to Long Beach and Tofino before the road was built in 1942. Learn and witness the aftermath of logging the ancient old growth that once stood along the trail.

18 **Half Moon Bay Trail.** Easy 1.7 km(1.06 mi). Best at low tide to view the many tidal pools. Wind through an ancient old growth forest, and witness the fallen trees that are now nurse logs offering nutrients/stability to baby seedlings. Passing cedar and hemlock, the trail down to Half Moon Bay Beach steepens and transforms into a forest of twisted cork-screwed spruce from winter storms. Some of the most beautiful vistas in the Pacific Rim.

19 **Tonquin Park.** Moderate 2.6 km(1.62 mi). The closest hiking area to town. If your partner is off shopping, this is a great beach to take the kids, and it is walking distance from downtown. Best to park in town and walk (10 minutes up 1st Street). Also, make sure to use the washroom and garbage facilities in town beforehand due to lack of amenities. Trailhead begins at the Community Hall.

Note: We do have secret trails, but they wouldn't be a secret if I published them in this book. Use these trails at your own risk, many are not maintained, with no markings. They keep Search & Rescue busy in the summer. For the more adventurous souls, feel free to ask around town and if you are lucky, perhaps a local will divulge.

Entertainment & Activities

20   **Visit Grice Bay**. To truly absorb the beauty of Tofino Inlet, drive straight down the road to Grice Bay where you can park near the water. Bring a couple of camping chairs and snacks, sit and enjoy. Normally used as a boat launch point, may have high activity in summer months. Great for picnics, reading, and has access to toilets.

21   **Visit the Kwisitis Visitor Centre.** A beautiful and free small museum featuring life-size exhibits of the local history, people and wildlife. Pick-up your Parks Canada Passes here as well. Enjoy a meal and watch the local surfers and waves crashing on Wickaninnish Beach from the **Kwisitis Feast House.** The Visitor Centre and Feast House are perched at the end of a rocky headland surrounded by ocean.

22   **Take a footprint picture in the sand.** A great way to remember your trip.

23   **Stock up on reusable items!** Grab a Tofino coffee mug (**Tofitian Café, Tofino Coffee Roasting Co.**), a cool re-usable water bottle, re-usable containers, thermos, cooler bag, cloth shopping bag etc. and see if you can go your entire trip without using one disposable cup, plastic water bottle, to go box, plastic shopping bag, single use item. These items double as souvenirs. Get used to saying "no straw please." Create a competition with the family - whoever goes the longest without using a single use plastic item wins! You and rivals can decide the prize. Make Tofitians proud! Tofino tip: Large wide mouth mason jars are great for many things!

24   **Jump in the water!** The ocean is your oyster. Please be aware that all beaches are unsupervised! We have no lifeguards, so you swim and surf at your own risk. Tofino's watersports are world famous. Make sure to suit up before hand, or for the hard-core soul in you do it in boardshorts or a bikini! Have a contest and see who of you can stay in the chilly Pacific for the longest.

25   **Take a surf lesson**. Suit up and hit the beach. Cold-water surfing has never been so popular! Tofino is Canada's prime surf destination. Before heading out, check out the live surf web cams at **Surfcam.ca. Surf Sister, Tofino Surf School, Pacific Surf School, Tofino Surf Adventures, Live to Surf, Westside Surf School, Bruhwiler Surf School** all offer lessons to kids and adults. I highly recommend first- timers to take a proper surf lesson. It will fast track your success to becoming the next professional surfer.

26   **Discover Stand Up Paddle Boarding (SUP).** Is surfing too challenging for you, but you want to still get out on the water? SUPing is your answer! This new and exciting sport has gained tremendous popularity within

the past decade. I highly recommend taking a lesson from **Tofino Paddle Surf** at MacKenzie Beach or **T'ashii Paddle School.** Eventually, when you become comfortable enough, try SUP surfing!

27 **Try SUPing (Stand Up Paddle Boarding) + Yoga = SUP YOGA!** *Dede Monette* is the SUP YOGA queen of Tofino and will teach you everything you need to know to get your downward dog down on a SUP floating on the ocean. The ultimate Tofino yoga experience. She also offers beach yoga, yoga retreats, bridal and kids yoga. www.tofinoyoga.com

28 **Go rock climbing**. Even though Tofino is not known to be a rock climbing destination, the avid experienced rock climbing addict can still find a few small gems. Head to Wya Beach or Tonquin at low tide for some fun little scrambles/boulder routes. South Beach, by Kwisitis, has some nice bouldering stacks. Florencia and Rosie Bay have some sea stacks and traverses you can play around on, but beware—the rock is sharp!

29 **Hit Long Beach at first light.** On a cooler morning you can hunt for spider webs! My friend Ivan always describes it as looking like a 'gypsy belt'. Watch the beauty of the dew off the webs and grass tips. Also watch and be mesmerized as the fog rises off the driftwood. Life is all about the simple things.

30 **Practice respect for all living things.** *"When I was leading traditional dugout canoe tours we'd often cross paths with various animals. Sometimes visitors would scare away the animals they were trying to watch by pointing at them. If you saw a little child that was shy,*

pointing at them would not help you get any closer. Most people and animals don't enjoy getting pointed at. There's a saying in our language that says, 'If you point at an eagle your finger will rot off.' It's taken me some practice to stop finger pointing, and I'm very lucky to still have my digits!" Gisele Maria Martin-Cultural Advocate, Tla-o-qui-aht First Nations.

31 **Bonfires, smores and spider dogs galore!** Pick up some firewood, never burn driftwood, and practice your beach fire making skills. Some great beaches for fires are South/ North Chesterman Beaches, MacKenzie Beach and Middle Beach. Make sure to check on local fire restrictions, and that you build your small fire below the high tide line. It also needs to be put out before 11:00 PM, and pack out what you pack in. Don't forget the guitar!

32 **Hot Springs Cove**. Set aside a good six to seven hours for this epic adventure! This is the ultimate Tofino experience. If you had only ONE day here, I'd recommend this. There are a number of charter companies in town that offer boat/plane rides to the Hot Springs Cove. Pack a lunch and enjoy the 20-minute scenic flight or a just over 1-hour boat ride, each way. Then it's a 30-minute hike through dense temperate rainforest to arrive at the famous hot spring pools that reach upwards to 50C (122F). The water flows from a small waterfall to five small pools that leads to the ocean. The best time to go is around high tide, and sometimes you'll have ocean waves busting into the pools below.

33 **Extend your Hot Springs experience by booking a**

night or two on the *Innchanter B&B*. This heritage house boat offers luxury accommodations with gourmet meals all while floating on the beautiful Hot Springs Cove.

34 **Cruise the inlets near Tofino aboard Tofino Water Taxi's Silent 1!** Tofino's brand new and very first zero emission electric charter boat. For more information, visit: www.tofinowatertaxi.com

35 **Bear Watching**. We love black bears! On low tide, watch bears as they come down to the protein market and forage for rock crab, sea stars, kelp, amongst many things. You'll most likely come across some of our other friends including eagles, porpoises, seals, river otters, blue herons, possibly a wolf and more. The best bear watching is between May-October.

36 **Whale watching**. Tofino still has a very pristine coastline where local and migratory whales come to feed throughout the year. Orcas roam all year. From March-September you'll find migrating Humpbacks who come to hang with the resident Gray whale. And from March to May its prime time. Up to 25,000 Gray whales pass through on their journey from Mexico to Alaska. Hop on a smaller zodiac, a ship with all amenities, or a floatplane for your whale seeking adventure.

37 **Charter a boat and explore the Sound**. Visit Cannery Bay and spend the afternoon. During the summer months, the warm waters of the Kennedy River flow into the Clayoquot Sound making it perfect for swimming.

38 Go tide pool exploring and see what sea life you can find! Tofino has some of the best tide pools in Canada! At low tide visit Crystal Cove, MacKenzie Beach, North Chesterman, Rosie Bay, or Combers Beach for prime tidal pool exploring. Try to identify all of the marine critters on the rocks at low tide.

39 Have a one-on-one professional surf coaching session with Shannon Brown, or Sepp Bruhwiler. This is for you if you are an intermediate-advanced surfer who wants to take your surfing up a notch. Shannon focuses on video analysis to help you get to the next level in your surfing. For more info, www.westsidesurf.com/private-surf-coaching.

40 Find the biggest tree you can find and give it a huge hug! A sure way to feel re-energized and put a smile on anyone's face. We are all tree huggers here.

41 Book a fun family or romantic couple photo session with one of our many local photographers. Make it outdoorsy/Tofino style, a nice memory you can take with you.

42 Have a First Nations Eco-Cultural Experience! Join Spirit Eagle Experiences for a guided lifetime experience. Experience the Ahousaht First Nations culture, their home and what they do today. Exchange stories with elders, local artists and singers. Enjoy traditional Indigenous foods. Gather seafood, harvest hystuup from the reefs and fish for the tyee. Explore the Ahousaht Hahoothee for spiritual connections, eagles, whales & other local happenings. For more information, visit: www.spiriteagle.ca

43 **Stay at Vera's Guest House or the Aauuknuk Lodge on beautiful Flores Island.** It's open year round for an Ahousaht Cultural Experience. Vera, a super friendly member of the Ahousaht community, will cook your meals and treat you to a unique experience on the West Coast. Aauunknuk Lodge is an ecological, sustainable, ecotourism operation and will enlighten your understanding of the rich culture and history of the Ahousaht First Nation. For more information, visit: www.aauuknuklodge.com

44 **Learn about Cougar Annie and visit her garden in Hesquiat Harbour**. A heritage site that endured 100 years, resurrected from a thick tangle of salal, scotch broom, and salmonberry. The garden sits on five-acres with over 2 km(1.24 mi) of crisscrossing pathways. For more information, visit: www.boatbasin.org

45 **Stop by the *Pacific Rim Visitor Center* at the Junction, or Greenpoint Campground next to Long Beach.** You'll find valuable information on things to do and see in the Pacfic Rim National Park. Parks Canada offers many educational sessions throughout the season for people of all ages to enjoy. Greenpoint Campground boasts a beautiful theater. Pick up information booklets or drop into one of their bear, wolf, cougar presentations to learn more about local wildlife and habitat.

46 **Yoga and Meditation on the beach.** Grab a towel, pick a beach, tune out, and get your zen on. There are a number of beach yoga classes offered as well throughout the high season through **Coastal Bliss Yoga.**

47 Skateboard/longboard/BMX/rollerblade/scooter. Or make up your own wheelie sport and cruise the **Tuff City Skate Park.** This is one of the most user friendly skate parks in Canada and probably the only one that doesn't sport any crazy graffiti. For all ages. In Tofino you could be 10 years old or 45, we all like to hit up the skate park once in a while. Everyone is welcome!

48 Rent a mountain bike and hit up the *Tuff City Bike Park.* It's just up near Tonquin Park. A well maintained dirt and wooden track with jumps to practice your mountain bike/BMX skills.

49 Try a Zumba class or one of the many *other weekly classes at the Tofino Community Hall!* You are guaranteed to be breaking a sweat and learning some new steps. Go solo, there are always extra solo dancers, or bring a partner. Whatever you do, work up a sweat having fun doing it. For more information, visit: www.tofino.ca/content/tofino-recreation-programs.

50 Want to know your future? Speak with the other side? Tofino psychic, Kate Sitka, offers guidance. A spirit medium and animal communicator, she'll do in-person sessions in her home or on the beach. Make sure to book three months in advance. www.tofinopsychic.com

51 Be healed by *Thérèse Bouchard* or *Deb Hillier.* Thérèse, a long-time resident (easily recognizable by her wild curly mane of dark brown almost black locks) uses a variety of techniques, including Massage Hypnotherapy, to help people in their quest for well-being. Deb Hillier specializes in channeling, usui reiki, tarot readings, and teachings on crystal healing, balancing chakras, and developing intuition.

52 **Go kayaking!** There are many local companies that offer guided tours and kayak rentals. ***Tofino Sea Kayaking*** is great. You can tour the inlet with one of their experienced guides, or rent a kayak yourself if you are experienced/ knowledgeable of the area. Sip an espresso before heading out enjoying the view from their waterfront patio, or browse their lovely shop.

53 **Get familiar with our Multi-Use Path (MUP)** by renting a bike. Proper etiquette: yield to walkers/ runners, stick to the right lane at all times, and use your bell and yell "passing to the left" when passing. Watch for hidden driveways, and wear a headlamp after dark. Dogs must be on a leash and under control at all times. Make sure to always secure your bike, especially during the summer months.

54 **Pamper yourself.** Indulge in massage therapy treatments, body scrubs, facials and more. We are lucky to have world class spas right here in Tofino. Try a revitalizing acupuncture session with Arbutus Health Center, also offering massage, yoga, herbal dispensary. Loosening all those sore muscles after a long day of hikes or surfing with a well-deserved full body massage is a great way to end your fun-filled day.

55 **Open mike night and karaoke night at Jack's Pub.** Every Monday and Wednesday ***Jack's Pub*** gets wild. We have minimum nightlife here in Tofino, but these are the nights it really goes off. This is where you get to meet the locals.

56   **Mushrooms galore**. One reason why I love the rain is because it always brings juicy Chantrelle mushrooms! Head to the woods to find these delicacies. Always bring a GPS or compass; getting lost in the wild is no fun and quite dangerous! Before you head out, do ensure you know what you are doing or have an experienced guide/ local with you. Harvest sustainably by cutting above the root, so the next person or animal will have another mushroom to enjoy. Watch for the poisonous look alike Chanterelles. Best time to forage is August-October.

57   **Forage for wild fruit.** Tofino is home to many different delicious varieties of wild berries from raspberries, blackberries, gooseberries, huckleberries, salal berries. Why do you think black bears love it here! Head out and go on a berry picking frenzy. The search is the fun part.

58   **Pick up a wildlife tracking booklet.** These are available from the Pacific Rim National Park Reserve. See what tracks you can find and identify. Always respect wildlife, and give animals lots of space.

59   **Visit the Raincoast Education Society at the EcoLodge.** Located in the Tofino Botanical Gardens, they have an amazing educational book selection. They host a Speaker Series, Ecology Tours, the Tofino Ambassador Program, and many more educational programs. Learn how to tell the difference between these giants: Douglas Fur Tree, Western Hemlock Tree, Western Red Cedars, and a Sitka Spruce Tree. To find out more, visit www.raincoasteducation.org or www.facebook.com/raincoast.education

60 **Find a banana slug!** This is the largest slug in the world and can literally grow to the size of a banana. Keep your eyes peeled, because we have many in our Tofino Rainforest. These slugs love mushrooms, lichens, and herbs.

61 **Learn 10 important facts about our rainforest.** Learn what keeps it healthy before you leave. Spend at least a few hours in our canopied ancient forest.

62 **Visit the Botanical Gardens!** One of my favorite places, where you can enjoy some peace and quiet in the summertime. Take a guided nature tour. This 12-acre waterfront nature preserve showcases children's garden and programs *(Tofino Nature Kids),* walking trails, boardwalks, mudflats. They also have a small quaint café called Darwin's where you can sit out on the patio and absorb the surroundings.

63 **Go squid fishing at night!** Grab some jigging gear, and head down to the Crab Dock at the bottom of Olsen Road after dark. Squid mainly feed at night and are attracted to light, which is why the docks are great locations. They like young herring and other small fishes, often lurking in the dark patches of water waiting to dart into the brightness to catch their hunt. Take a camping lantern or flashlight for the unlit areas.

64 **Feeling artsy? Check out Tofino Art Council events.** At the *Common Loaf Bake Shop,* they often hold late Friday Art Party Nights for adults during the off-season. Art supplies provided, donations welcome.

65 **Catch a movie.** Every Monday Night is Movie Night

251 Things to Do in **Tofino**

in Tofino starting at 8:00 PM at the ***Clayoquot Sound Theater.*** We have our own movie theater! Enjoy Warren Rudd's Organic Snacks and check out the lineup of films at www.tofinomovies.blogspot.ca

66 **Go to the Whale Centre** and discover many Nuu-chah-nulth ancient artifacts, and an entire Gray Whale skeleton! They have a great little gift shop as well.

67 **Get out on the water and visit a neighboring oyster farm.** Learn how and where they grow, as well as how they are harvested from farm to your plate. More than 50,000 gallons (190,000L) of this special bivalve are harvested in Clayoquot Sound annually. November is Oyster Month! Fun fact: 1 oyster can filter over 50 gallons (200L) of water per day! November is oyster month.

68 **Take a scenic flight of Clayoquot Sound on a Floatplane or a Glacier Tour by helicopter or airplane.** From sea to mountain and back to sea. Cruise up to altitude and witness over 10,000 year old local glaciers. Deep inlets carpeted with ancient old growth lead up to these pristine snowy peaks of Strathcona Park. Experience the Sound in a unique way. Revel in the wonders of the beautiful temperate rainforest.

69 **Visit the Thornton Creek Hatchery,** Port Albion Road (10km/6.21mi from Ucluelet), to see and learn all about salmon. The best times to see adult spawning salmon is mid-October to November, and juveniles can be viewed March to June. From July to August, there are no fish on site, and limited staff. To book a tour, call 250-726-7566.

70 **Golfing.** Do you consider yourself a Golf Nut? We have a golf course here too! And it's pretty great. Whack some balls with the locals who frequent often and see who can get the best golf tan by the end of the day out at **Long Beach Golf Course,** which offers a 9-hole championship course, driving range, mini-golf, paintball, wilderness camping, cold beer, ice cream and a conference room.

71 **Go rainforest paintballing!** Yes, we have paintballing! Check out **Pacific Rim Woodsball,** located down near Long Beach Golf Course. They have gear for up to 20 players. Shoot between 500-1,500 eco-friendly paintballs, and your host will stay out for as long as you have the balls. For more information, visit: www.pacificrimwoodsball.com

72 **Experience ziplining!** Besides surfing, this is a great way to get your adrenaline pumping. Located in Ha`uukmin Tribal Park, **West Coast Wild** provides Zipline Eco Tours. The zipping route flies right over a beautiful river canyon and forest trails. Afraid of heights? The experienced local guides are with you every step of the way.

73 **Go river kayaking** in the calm waters of Kennedy River with West Coast Wild Eco Tour Adventure in Ha' uukmin Tribal Park. For more information, visit: www.wcwild.com

74 **Hooksum Outdoor School** is at Hesquiaht Harbour. Whether your group is interested in a quiet weekend retreat, an immersion into the natural and cultural history of Hesquiaht territories, an educational adventure investigating the ecosystems of Hesquiaht Harbour or a challenging week-long surfing adventure, at Hooksum, all sorts of learning takes place in the natural world. Local, knowledgeable and experienced guides and educators help everyone to get the most of their experience. For more information, visit: www.hooksumschool.com

75 **Play a game of bocce, volleyball, soccer, Frisbee, baseball on the beach.** Need games/equipment? Head to the Tofino Pharmacy or **Co-op Hardware Store** in town.

76 **Enjoy a nice picnic at the beach!** Stock up on goodies at **Picnic Charcuterie,** locally cured gourmet meats and cheeses, across from **Tofino Brew Co.,** where you can also grab some cold ones. Don't forget the beach blanket and sunscreen!

77 **Read at the beach.** Grab a beach blanket or camping chair and get comfy on the hot sand. Sit back, sunscreen up, and jump into a good book.

78 **Go topless or completely nude.** Hike down to Radar Hill Beach. Be careful; this hike is quite challenging and vertical. When you exit the forest at the bottom, to the left you'll find a large slow stream of freshwater (tastes great!) and in front a beautiful quiet sandy beach. The locals call this "Nude Beach[1]."

---

1   *http://tofinohostel.com/tofino*

79   **Hunt for sea biscuits!** Aka sand dollars. Did you know that sand dollars on our West Coast are completely different from the sand dollars on the East Coast (Atlantic Ocean)? Notice that the flower pattern is uneven (looking more like a hemp leaf, west coast style) due to the little guy anchoring himself on the sand bottom at an angle taking advantage of the current bringing goodies to him.

80   **Hunt for critters.** Grab a seaside book or woodland book and go for a critter hunt at the beach or in the woods. The mudflats are excellent critter hunting grounds. Be gentle and you'll make friends.

81   **Write messages in the sand.** Be creative and sketch wise words in the sand for a great photo op or for the next beachcomber to stumble upon your message.

82   **Sunsets sunsets sunsets.** Tofino is home to some of the most beautiful sunsets in the world. Every time I witness these spectacular paintings in the sky, each one is unique and special. Try and keep a Tofino sunset photo log while you are here.

83   **Build a sandcastle.** Google for ideas, and get creative. They aren't just for kids. Or build a drift wood fort, Long Beach is a perfect spot for this.

84   **Learn how to perfectly fillet a wild salmon and how to BBQ it to perfection.** This is a very important skill here on the West Coast; everyone should know how to fillet a salmon and cook it properly. Salmon cooking is an art, and there are many ways to do it.

85 **Hunt for a sea urchin and try this local favorite delicacy raw!** Make sure there is no red tide in the area beforehand. Sea urchin is super healthy for you, and for the local Nuu-chah-nulth it has been a staple in their diet for thousands of years. You'll need your saltwater fishing license, or best, a licensed guide with you.

86 **Forage for mussels and clams!** You are allowed to forage for mussels and clams year-round. Check that there are no red tides in the area. You can find these tasty molluscs on beaches near tidal mudflats, and if you plan to go without a licensed guide, make sure to pick up a saltwater fishing license, if you don't already have one.

87 **Buy a Shucking Knife in town, find some fresh unshucked oysters, and learn how to shuck!** You can buy unshucked oysters from any of the seafood stores in town such as *The Fish Store* 368 Main St. (no website), *Trilogy Fish Co.* (www.trilogyfish.net)

88 **Pick up a copy of "The SOBO Cookbook" by owner/chef Lisa Ahier** and learn how to cook a proper Dungeness crab or how to whip up yummy West Coast Ceviche. **SoBo** has always been loved by locals, and in many local Tofitian kitchens you are bound to come across a copy of this "Tofitian Food Bible."

89 **Take a nap on the beach.** String a hammock between two trees if you can find a good place, or simply bring a blanket and even a pillow if you like. Kick-back and relax. Take in the sounds of the ocean, as you dream of orcas, sea lions, gray whales, sea birds, mermaids, canoes, shipwrecks and ancient sailors.

90 **Make a fun earthquake kit with your family/ friends and donate it to a local family before you leave.** It's always great to be prepared! And it's a great learning experience for all ages, kids and adults. Plus, that local family will really appreciate your gift. For more information, visit: www.totallyunprepared.com/ make-a-home-earthquake-ki/

91 **Are you feeling artsy? Find an old surfboard or a broken one and paint it as the ultimate souvenir of your Tofino memories.** You can find paints at the local Co-op Hardware store and the Tofino Pharmacy.

92 **Learn about local permaculture, sustainability, being green** by booking a session with local permaculturist Ariel Novak. Contact him at *permaculturetofino@gmail.com*

93 **Pick-up a FREE copy of our local monthly *Tofino Time Magazine*** for all the up-to-date weekly events in Tofino and Ucluelet. This is my favorite magazine (besides Surfer) because it always has cool local stories, astrology and keeps you in the loop on fun things around town.

94 **Grab a copy of the new *LATER Magazine* and *Coast Mountain Culture Magazine*.** This is a must for all those die hard surfers out there and outdoor enthusiasts. LATER magazine can be found at any of the local surf shops. It's all about getting mugged, getting barrelled, travelling, music, and generally having a good time. Coast Mountain Culture Magazine you'll find in many of the cafes/shops, and it is free.

95 **Go on a garbage beach cleanup frenzy!** Grab a garbage bag or two and head out with the kiddies or your partner and collect garbage up and down a local beach. Watch for treasures! Drop the collected garbage in any of the local public bins at the beach parking, or in town. Take a photo and tag @surfrider @surfriderpacificrim #tofino #surfriderpacificrim.

96 **Wetsuit races.** Hanging around the beach? Yell "WETSUIT RACE!" grab all your mates and race to a chunk of driftwood, rock, seaweed patch, you name it. Sand diving encouraged, just make sure your mouth is closed!

97 **Surf looks pumping?** Watch from the beach and see if you can find local rippers/professional surfers Pete Devries, Michael Darling or Noah Cohen out in the water putting on an aerial show. Flying left, right, and center!

98 **Get Married!** There are more than 200 weddings per year here in Tofino! That's almost one a day! We are almost the Vegas of the North, so why not get hitched? Go visit Sheila at *Rare Earth Weddings* in the Shore Building on Main Street.

99 **Visit Freedom Cove, a giant floating home!** Local artists Catherine and Wayne Adams will guide you through their fully sustainable, off the grid sanctuary deep in the heart of Clayoquot Sound. A truly unique, awe-inspiring experience! Contact freedomcove4@gmail.com. For more information, visit: www.browningpass.com/freedom-cove-tour-tofino

100 **Go Fishing!** Tofino is a fisherman's paradise. I highly recommend not leaving until you have done a sportfishing excursion through one of our many excellent charter companies. Experienced local guides will take you to offshore or inshore waters where you'll most likely reel in a big catch, possibly even fill your freezer. There's also remote freshwater excursions offered for the much prized steelhead, rainbow and cutthroat trout that are catch and release. Or take the whole family on one of the many family friendly excursions. Ask your guide about smoking your fresh caught salmon locally or having a local chef cook up your catch for dinner.

101 **Bird watch on the famous rich mudflats!** Clayoquot Sound is home to some of the richest protected habitats in the world. Countless feathered species come as guests to feed and rest upon our vast protein rich mudflats as they migrate from Mexico to Alaska from April to May. Grab a pair of binoculars and hit the mudflats to view many different species of birds, both migratory and local. Bring a bird book and try your luck at identifying the numerous special, beautiful species.

102 **Feeling adventurous and want to be highly active? Bike the straight Pacific Rim Highway to Ucluelet,** The Multi-Use Path (MUP) will take you as far as Cox Bay Information Center and begins again after the junction arriving into Ucluelet. It takes less than two hours to bike the entire length from Tofino to Ucluelet each way, 40 km(24.85 mi). Be very careful when biking on the highway and always wear a bike helmet! An easier option would be to turn around at Long Beach which takes less than an hour one way. Happy cycling!

103 **Body surfing, Boogie Boarding, Skim Boarding...** Just get out there! Pick up a cool hand-made wooden hand plane from Storm Surf Shop. These neat hand planes enable you to glide across waves with a small board on the end of your arm. Pure surfer and wave bro, really cool. Plus, it's easier to get barreled this way, because of the smaller swell especially during the summer months. You're more compact thus easier to pull into little green rooms.

104 **Kiteboarding.** Bring your own gear, and hit North or South Chesterman Beach on a windy onshore day (perfect because it's usually horrible surf conditions!) for some excellent kiteboarding.

105 **Play a soccer game at the school field, or throw a football or Frisbee** with friends or family. School is out in the summer! Check first to see if the big grassy field is free behind the school at the top end of 4th Street.

106 **Play some beach hockey!** Bring your sticks and play a game of beach hockey! (There is such a thing.) You just need a larger ball and actual hockey sticks or field hockey sticks, or be creative and find some driftwood hockey sticks!

107 **Hit the gym!** For those who still need to pump the iron everyday and do some push-ups squats elliptical the **Tofino Fitness Center** has a 24/7 small gym facility equipped with bathrooms/showers.

108 **Head to the 1st Street Dock.** Grab some snacks

from the **Tofino Co-op,** pull up to a picnic table at the waterfront and watch as the seaplanes take off and land, the fishing boats come and go, eagles swoop, Mr. Otter swimming amongst the kelp beds, and more. There's so much to see!

109 **Crash a beach fire!** Don't have a beach fire? No problem. Grab a bunch of cold ones, walk down MacKenzie, North or South Chesterman Beach and ask to join a fire, generously offering wood or beverages in return of course. Fire curfew is 11PM, make sure to spread out the wood or use water to put the fire out. Never cover with sand because kids can walk on it the next day. Take out what you take in. This is a great way to make new friends.

110 **Fly a kite.** Kites are for adults too, and it is a great way to spend a nice sunny, windy day at the beach!

111 **Get out on the water in a traditional Nuu-chah-nulth dugout canoe with T'ashii Paddle School.** Born and raised local Tla-o-qui-aht Tsimka Martin gives eco tours on large traditional dugout canoes that are handcrafted by her father and uncle. Absorb the tranquility of Clayoquot Sound, without the sound of a motor behind you, and listen to animal stories, legends, traditional teachings, and as she talks about the history of the area. Her guided walks and canoe tours are oil free!

112 **Catch a full moon.** Do what the locals do and head for a full moon surf at North or South Chesterman Beach, or go stand up paddle boarding at MacKenzie Beach, or just walk the beach dipping your feet in the water while witnessing the natural light show of phytoplankton bioluminescence. **Dance in the moonlight!** Tofitians love their full moons and new moons, and many believe in moon superstitions. Look up common moon superstitions and see what you believe, or test it out!

113 **Practice your photo skills.** Grab a film camera and fill it with Tofino shots; sunsets, smiles, wildlife critters, trees of the rainforest, and sand monsters. Make an easy waterproof camera: plastic bag + disposable camera (just in case it leaks). Developing your shots after your return home will be the best part of re-living your Tofino experience.

114 **Be a professional beach bum for the length of your stay!** Set your goal as living up to the official definition of a beach bum - "someone who spends most of his or her time having a good time on the beach." (Definition of beach bum from the Cambridge Advanced Learner's Dictionary & Thesaurus © Cambridge University Press)

115 **Welcome to the Love Shack...** Tofino can quite possibly be called unofficially "Canada's Love Capital" (plus many other capitals). Get your love on in many ways. You can start by writing your initials and your partner's in the sand with a heart.

116 **Practice finding pleasure** in everything you do during your stay. Slow down, unwind, be mindful and appreciate the little things in life, such as the feel of sand between your toes, the smell of the salt in the air, all of the surrounding sounds…from the distant float planes taking off/landing, the calls of the great blue heron or eagle, to the pitter-patter of the raindrops.

117 **Live and Die by the Tide.** Let the tide rule you for a day or two. Plan your surfs, beach explorations, naps, kayak excursions, hotsprings tour etc. by the tidal times. Beach explorations are usually best at low tide. Waves for surfing are better on the rising tide. Prime kayaking or stand up paddle boarding times on the inlet are best at slack tides (at peak high or peak low). The hotsprings are most enjoyable at higher tides.

118 **Calling all Sun Worshippers, Bronze Queens and Kings!** Soak up some Tofino rays on those bright sunny days as you lay in the warm sand and relax. Don't forget the coconut oil!

119 **Grab a blanket, and head to the beach/backyard patio for a long stargazing session.** Warning: this will be a soul changing experience. Fall asleep under the stars. Every August 10-11th witness the annual meteor showers.

120 **Bringing it back old school and tune into 90.1 FM and listen to Tofino's very own *Tuff City radio station!*** When was the last time you listened to the radio? We love our radio station! Local interviews and great music bring the community closer together. Guest speakers are highly welcomed. Tell us what you love about Tofino.

121 **Try to distinguish all the calls of nature!** Find out what an eagle cry sounds like! Or a wolf! A bear! An orca! Mr. Crow at **Wildside Grill!** Aim to have an ear for nature before you leave.

122 **Lay in the hot sand, close your eyes, take a**

deep breath, and inhale the sweet smells for a few minutes…or an hour or two.

123 **Start or continue writing your masterpiece!** There's a reason Tofino has a very high number of writers per capita. Get comfortable and let your mind run wild as you write down your words. Let the environment, nature, inspire you. Be careful, inspiration overload is common in Tofino.

124 **Have a digital detox!** Do what you gotta do, put a pillow over it and head out! Leave the electronics at home for a day or try a week and just be present in the moment. The way life should be.

125 **Be a pirate and go on a treasure hunt!** Go to *www.geocaching.com* for directions to a few Tofino treasures. All you need is to sign up and load the coordinates into your smart phone or GPS to find the hidden locations.

126 **Want to get Fit to Rip?** Our friend Nicole Lohse, offers a series of 6 fitness lessons designed specifically around the movements you do while surfing, focusing on land-based training techniques. For more info and to book a session, visit www.fittorip.com

127 **Take a remote surf trip with local surf legend Raph Bruhwiler.** Sick of crowds, want to get out more into the wild, and surf remote beaches? This is for you. For more information, visit: www.bruhwilersurf.com

128 Be the next Steven Spielberg, but Steve Irwin style and grab your GoPro and start shooting! **Create an epic Tofino film** in and out of the water.

129 **Make yourself prettier! Get a hair-do or your nails done** (maybe a cool Tofino ocean theme!) *Studio One Aveda Concept Salon, Salty Dolls Hair Salon, Best Little Hair House,* or *Petrichor Hair Workshop.*

130 **Discover the art of strolling and people watching** around town with numerous sidewalk benches to park yourself. My favorite is the one in front of *Tuff Beans Cafe* or the busy sidewalk outside of *Rhino Coffee House.*

131 **Be the first person in the water before sunrise.** Being the first in the water is always a special feeling. Suit up and race to the water to warm up. The moment you bath yourself in the coolness you are instantly awakened, no coffee needed. You'll have all the waves to yourself until the sleepy town catches up to you.

132 **Be the last person out of the water after sunset.** Watch as the sun slowly melts into the horizon and the moon becomes brighter. Sunsets are my favorite time to surf because the water usually has this oil slick look to it with colors of the sky turning the gray to different shades of pink, purple and orange.. You have VIP seating to some of the best sunsets. Once the sun dips below the horizon, catching waves can be a little more challenging which is the fun part! Be patient to make your last wave one of the best. Cheers to a great day!

133 **Get to know all the names of the peaks that you see across the Tofino Inlet plus the traditional Tla-o-qui-aht names.** Which one is Catface Mountain? Lone Cone? You'll impress any local with this knowledge.

134 **Plan ahead and make your MUST DO LIST for your next visit.**

135 **Get a tattoo** by long-time local Tofitian Danby Russell White at ***Tuff City Pricks Tattoo.*** facebook.com/DanbyRussell There's also ***End o the Road Tattoo*** on 4th Street, opened seasonally.

Tofino Food & Drink

We are absolutely spoiled rotten with amazing gourmet food at our fingertips as Tofitians.

136 **Coffee Fanatics Tour.** Tofino is the place to go on a coffee crawl! See where you can find the best cup of local java. Tofino is known for having great coffee; welcome to the land of coffee snobs. Many Tofitians start their day with a strong cup of organic coffee. Start at the far end of town at the local hot spot the ***Common Loaf Bake Shop,*** next the secret gem ***Tofino Sea Kayaking, Rhino Coffeehouse,*** the ***Wolf in the Fog, Tuff Beans, Tofino Coffee Co., Tofitian Café*** and the ***Driftwood Café at the Wick.***

137 **Try a little taste of Mexico in Tofino at the TacoFino Cantina** at the back of Beaches Plaza. Open every day 11:00 am to 8:00 pm in the summer. Try the fish tacos or pulled pork burritos. Enjoy homemade salsas and guacamole, and finish off with a spiced chocolate diablo cookie. Sip on their watermelon basil slushy while you wait.

138 **SoBo Restaurant** is famous amongst locals for their hand-squeezed key lime margaritas. Dine outside in front of the outdoor fireplace in the fall. What began as a food truck is now one of Tofino's top restaurants! Pick up *Lisa Ahier's cookbook* during your visit to bring SoBo home with you. Brunch, lunch and dinner. Delicious vegetarian and seafood options with a unique home style twist. Sick of seafood? Try their Thai chicken roti.

139 **Kuma Japanese Cuisine** offers comfort style Japanese food, making it a small quaint local favorite. After a cold surf, or day out on the water, warm up to a big bowl of udon or ramen noodle or order their take out Clayoquot seaweed bowl. Dinner only. Enjoy Kuma Happy Hour between 4:00 and 5:00 pm. Hot sake and shared dish specials. It's absolutely delicious and my favorite winter spot!

140 **Chef Mare Bruce of the Schooner Restaurant** will surely satisfy your belly with her fabulous West Coast dishes with an international twist. You cannot leave Tofino without trying her Admiral's Plate, the almighty God of seafood dishes. Her two sons, Whalen and Gray, daughter-in-law Jess run the show at the front, and you may spot little Dia, Mare's granddaughter, running around in her princess dress. Although she's just a little girl, she shares Mare's passion for cooking delicious food. The restaurant, an historic site, is also haunted with local resident ghost Maurice, an old time family friend who was the chowder man of the restaurant.

141 **Enjoy the best sushi in town at Tough City Sushi on the waterfront.** Make sure to say hi to Crazy Ron who sourced all of the recycled materials to build the "Victorian old looking" restaurant and inn. Check out all of his knick knacks! So cool. His son Lance is one of the chefs, but they have always had Japanese chefs. Menu favorites are the Smiling Buddha Roll, the Tofino Roll, and the local wild salmon and tuna sashimi. Also try the fresh Clayoquot Kushi oysters with a unique Japanese marinade. They also have the best chocolate mousse!

142 **Storm watch from The Pointe Restaurant** at the world class Wickaninnish Inn. The restaurant alone is a masterpiece, dotted with artwork, hand carved beams constructed by late master carver Henry Nola, with panoramic ocean views of North Chesterman Beach. Drop in for a gourmet breakfast made from scratch (even the butter is homemade!), while enjoying beautiful views. Dinner service; reservations required. An ever-changing menu with fresh seasonal ingredients. Open breakfast, lunch, and dinner.

143 **Walk Chesterman Beach and stop in at the Driftwood Café** at the Wickanninish Inn for a warm latte and fresh baked scones. The café has a very homely, comfortable feel making it easy to relax as you sip your coffee near the beach. Open breakfast, lunch, and dinner.

144 **What happens when a pack of very talented ex-Pointe Restaurant employees come together to create something out of pure passion?** The **Wolf in the Fog** comes alive. Chef Nick Nutting loves to fish, forage and cook with those same locally sourced West Coast ingredients. Meet the wonderful Hailey, one of the best bartenders in town, and share one of her punch bowls with a partner. Try their burger, their famous Truffle Potato Crusted Oysters, and one of their delicious Shared Dishes.

145 **Beaches Grocery Store** located near North Chesterman Beach known as 'Beaches Plaza' or Outside Break is a small quaint grocery store, but don't let its size trick you. They have almost everything! Try the warm, freshly baked muffins that are brought in every morning from Jupiter Juice. They also carry locally produced 600 Degrees Brick Oven Bakery breads.

146 **The Great Room at Long Beach Lodge Resort** is probably the comfiest place to hang out, especially in the winter time where you can watch the huge waves roll and crash into Cox Bay. Sit next to the fire place and enjoy a warm meal. Great place to grab brunch with the light streaming into the large windows, people watch from the window at Cox Bay beach, Canada's premier surf beach. Head down to their *Sandbar Bistro* during those warm days to enjoy a cold beverage near the beach.

147 **One of the best places to enjoy a sunset in Tofino, the Ice House Oyster Bar** on the dock has an excellent, simple seafood menu with fresh shucked local oysters. Don't mind the humming noise coming from the dock; it only adds to the character of the place. You can't get any closer to the water here. Grab a blanket to watch the sunset. Open seasonally.

148 **Chocolate Tofino for homemade chocolate and handmade gourmet ice cream.** Locals look forward to a power outage, which may happen once or twice during the summer, to get 50% off ice cream. Try their Salted Caramel Sundae! Owners Kim and Cam are delightful. "We never use artificial flavors, colors, or preservatives. Instead, we seek to incorporate organic and local flavors into our artisan chocolates. Highest quality ingredients. All of our delicious gelato and sorbet is also churned fresh in house from whole ingredients blended with natural flavors and is sure to please even the most discerning palette."

149 **Tofino Coffee Roasting Co.** The first coffee roasting company in Tofino! Also sold at the Co-op Grocery Store. Great coffee, simple, quick and easy...don't go to their quaint small café expecting much more. Supposedly the best coffee in Tofino...I'll leave it up to you to decide. Sit on the steps outside and watch the people stream in and out of town.

150 **Picnic Charcuterie.** "We cure, smoke and cook all our meats in-house emphasizing Vancouver Island and BC grown and harvested ingredients." Try their orange walnut pork sausage, amongst other cured treats and gourmet cheeses. A great place to grab a snack for your hot springs trip or beach picnic.

151 **Head to the Tofitian Cafe, one of my favourite places to grab a coffee,** to find cool swag with skull and cross bone surfboards, badass. Sip on your java outside in their enclosed forested outdoor sitting area while checking the bulletin board for events and festivals. Cash only.

152 **Tofino Brew Co.** Hang out in their tasting room, a popular local hangout, and try a plank of four draught beers. Pick up some Tofino Brew Co. swag while you're at it and look like a local! Pint size too small? Growl and grab a growler (refillable glass jug) to take home some delicious craft beer. Open from 11:00 am until 9:00 pm every day. Be sure to catch co-owner Dave Woodward aka Brewery Dave with his toque and bushy blonde hair.

153 **For fresh fish to cook up yourself, head to The Fish Store & Oyster Bar on Main.** If you are lucky the lovely co-owner Marcy with her luscious, blonde, curly mane will be there to entertain. Husband Lutz Ziliken, owns Tofino's West Pacific Seafoods, which supplies local fresh seafood to many local restaurants, and comes from a family of professional fishermen and fish smokers. The best fresh oysters served on half shell in town and some of the best smoked salmon dishes. Locals call the joint from *Schooner Restaurant* to *Tough City Sushi* to the *Oyster Bar* the Tofino Bermuda Triangle.

154 **Head to Trilogy Fish Co.** for more fresh local catch to cook up on the BBQ, at the beach, or at your vacation rental.

155 **If you are in a hurry and want tasty reasonably healthy takeaway fresh seafood head to the Wildside Grill.** Sit down and enjoy their outdoor picnic tables, but watch for Mr. Crow. Any bit of food left unattended will be snatched up as soon as you turn your back. They have the best salmon burger in town! Try it with a side of fresh mixed green salad or their homemade crispy fries. Jeff Mikus co-owner and commercial fishermen brings in the freshest catch daily from that morning.

156 **Middle Beach Lodge, a hidden large gem.** Although they do not advertise as a restaurant, you can certainly make reservations ahead of time if you have a larger group for dinner. The high end rustic lodge and surrounding cabins are built from salvaged wood, and it sits on 40 acres of secluded oceanfront land. Absolutely stunning!

157 **Do you like authentic Caribbean Cuisine? Try Calypso Roti Shop,** dine in and take-out on the waterfront. Great for vegans! Located down near the end of Main Street at the waterfront. Curry, jerk chicken and doubles (delicious Caribbean street food)! www.calypsorotishop.com

158 **Check out the new Monster Noodle Bar** on Main St., for tasty inexpensive Asian fusion noodles. If you need a quick bite, here's a good spot to grab and go. They have authentic kimchee and a number of spices on hand to dress up your noodles as well.

159 **Gary's Kitchen is Tofino's only Chinese restaurant.** Western Chinese fusion with a West Coast twist. This is a local hotspot. Try their Halibut Veggie Stir Fry or Salt and Pepper Squid. Hot big bowls of soup to warm up after those cold surf sessions.

160 **Red Can Gourmet everything they make is delicious and soul warming from their chowder, pizzas, gourmet sandwiches and pre-made salads!** Everything is created by a team of great people who go out of their way to provide an excellent meal at a great price. Grab a gourmet sandwich before heading out on any Clayoquot Sound adventure. Now serving an excellent brunch along with espresso. Fast, convenient, gourmet health foods.

161 **Tony's Pizza. Tiring day of surfing or travelling?** Get pizza delivered from Tony's. Tofino's classic pizza joint offering pizza by the slice as well. Dine in and sit in the tiny restaurant while watching a retro surf movie.

162 **Shelter Restaurant is another local hotspot, especially for the surfers.** A great place to chill out after a long adventurous day in and around the water. Catch up with friends and family and enjoy a delicious gourmet West Coast meal by Chef Matthew Kane. Try their local mussels and frites while watching a surf flick/ hockey game. Winter Canuck hockey nights with cheap $3 beers from the Tofino Brew Co.

163 **Big Daddy's Fish Fry.** This is a Tofino burger lover's paradise…if you are craving a big juicy fish burger (halibut, tuna, cod, salmon, prawn), beef or chicken, this is the place to go. Finish off with a yummy soft serve ice cream or milkshake pick and choose from 25 different flavors. Cash only.

164 **Rhino Coffee House is always a busy hangout spot.** Homemade fresh donuts to die for. Gluten free friendly. Try their breakfast burrito and their bacon maple donut if you are feeling experimental.

165 **Green Soul Organics offers fresh locally sourced organic produce, healthy snack foods,** and you can usually find any specialty health food item here with very helpful knowledgeable staff. It's right on the corner of Campbell and Neil beside **Wolf in the Fog.**

166 **Check out Earth Mama Love Kitchen Collective.** A vegan's dream! A unique group of people coming together offering fresh tasty organic food and drink, catering, workshops and more. Hot soups, warm dishes, salads, green poutine, fresh pressed juices, always vegetarian, usually vegan. Located in Green Soul Organics Grocery.

167 **Dockside Smoked Fish Store** sells an excellent variety of fresh smoked salmon in Tofino. Pick and choose from 19 varieties of smoked fish. Located in the House of Himwitsa, at the end of First Street.

168 **Tuff Beans Coffee House.** If it's a nice sunny morning, their patio is the perfect hang-out spot to enjoy a yummy breakfast burrito or a cold beer in the afternoon. A popular local breakfast joint with great staff!

169 **Darwin's Café.** Indeed, a getaway from the crowds with free chicken watching. Opened seasonally, enjoy organic espresso and baked goods away from the noisy town center while sitting out on their tranquil patio overlooking the beautiful Botanical Gardens. www.tbgf.org

170 **Jack's Greenroom Diner** is great for pancakes or a classic good value American style breakfast! The closest thing to a '50s diner with the added west coast waterfront view.

171 **Jack's Pub Marina West.** The one and only rough

around the edges pub in town. Classic deep fried goodness. Try their fresh fish tacos or the halibut burger with yam fries.

172 **Jamie's Rainforest.** Great breakfast. Live music every Tuesday and Sunday night from 9:00 to 11:00 pm, cheap beers. Bi-monthly comedy shows. Wednesday wing night. Friday industry night cheap nachos and Lucky Beer. Excellent menu filled with seafood selections, pastas, burgers, appetizers. For updated specials + events visit: www.tofinorainforestinn.com.

173 **The Sea Shanty** has one of the best inlet views in town. Enjoy their revamped menu of warm hearty seafood delights while taking in the breathtaking scenery of Clayoquot Sound.

174 **Tin Wis Beachfront Bistro.** Great breakfast, for a good price with views of MacKenzie Beach. Grab a bite, and head out for a beach walk only steps away.

175 **Common Loaf Bake Shop, the original Tofino bakery** serving the widest selection of fresh baked goods in Tofino as well as many gluten free options. The Loaf, as locals call it, is not only a café but a community. Head up their winding, narrow stairs and sit out on the upper balcony soaking up some sun rays. Watch out for those sneaky ravens. Try their breakfast sandwich! Cash only.

176 **The Sugar Shack and the Candy Jar.** Craving sweets? Open seasonally with a great selection.

** Too relaxed? Want to stay in? Order from **Tofino Delivery**; food from a number of local restaurants or liquor right to your doorstep. Service 'til 11PM most days. For more info, visit **www.deliveryscoots.com**.*

Tofino Art & Artists

Our artistic, nature-inspired community supports and encourages old and new art forms and continually uplifts people to tap into their creative souls. Tofino Clayoquot Sound attracts many artists from all across the nation. Art is planted very strongly in the roots of the local Nuu-cha-nulth and local Tofitians.

177 **Fill your day with local art obsession!** Create a daylight version of the famous Nuit Blanche by parading about town visiting art gallery after art gallery.

178 **Visit the House of Himwitsa Native Art Gallery,** it's also a lodge and a dockside smoked fish store. Owners Lewis and Cathy George, came up with the name Himwitsa from local elders, which translates to "story telling and the passing of knowledge from elder to youth." Here you'll find beautiful carvings, masks, jewellery, hand-knit goods, First Nation's artwork handcrafted by some of the region's most talented and innovative native artists.

179 **The Village Gallery** is a small, quaint Tofino gallery on 321 Main Street with a vast collection of limited editions, prints, cards and much more.

180 **Check out Kevin Midgley's Tofino Art Glass Studio** at 264 First Street. Eccentric handmade glass pieces, earrings, pendants, plates, bowls and art pieces handmade in Tofino. Beach sand surfer pendants. Enroute to Tonquin Park. Open most days, most of the time, but open when open and closed when closed.

181 **Kate Koreski Jewelry.** Kate's studio/shop at 210 First Street is open seasonally. A born and raised Tofitian, she draws inspiration from the culture, style and fashion of the women of South America, specifically Buenos Aires.

182 **Check out Merge, an artisan collective behind the CIBC.** Owners Laurie and Victoria have recently opened this shop of carefully selected handmade goods, mostly local, and created a space for artists. See Marcus Paladino and Adam Chilton Photography, Marion Syme Illustrations, Market Canvas Leather, Lisa Fletcher and Highwaters Jewellery, and much more.

183 **Step into Roy Henry Vickers, Eagle Aerie Gallery.** Roy is a prominent First Nations artist recognized for his carvings, paintings and prints. Built in 1986 with the help of Roy's family and legendary carver Henry Nolla, this gallery welcomes more than 500,000 visitors a year from all around the world.

184 **Love Craft (346 Campbell Street)** This is a great place to grab an Italian coffee, and owner Cory specializes in textiles. His gallery features many unique handmade creations from local West Coast artists as well as fashionable clothing.

185 **Mark Hobson's Gallery for his underwater paintings, limited edition reproductions, gift shop items,** such as art cards and calendars. Mark is best known for his portrayals of wildlife and Canadian West Coast landscapes. From rainforests to the underwater realm, from pounding surf to misty coves, the careful use of light is always present enhancing subtle drama in his work.

186 **Rubio has a great collection of locally hand crafted jewellery in silver and gold** made with some of BC's precious gems and local stones. Large selection of First Nations gold and silver jewellery on the West Coast, also First Nations art and hand carved masks.

187 **Love the smell of cedar? Visit the Tofino Cedar Furniture Shop and Show Patio at 671 Industrial Way** next to Long Beach Automotive. Specializing in locally made, hand crafted, sustainable, solid cedar Adirondack furniture. www.tofinocedarfurniture.com

188 **SALT Tofino Lifestyle & Giftshop above the Whale Centre** features local handcrafted goods, from wooden iPhone covers, Tofino Soap, local print shirts, jewellery, Tofino Woodworks, and more.

189 **Lisa Fletcher Jewellery** is all handcrafted metal and gemstone jewelry from her own studio in Tofino. You can tell that each piece is connected to the surrounding environment where it was made. Available at ***Rubio, Caravan Beach Shop, Wickaninnish Inn,*** and the Wedding Store.

190 **House of Alaia** is a place created by Nea Hildebolt and Christy Feaver to bring people together to explore their creative sides. Adults and children can come to explore creation through jewelry making and art. Offering classes for everyone from beginner to advanced. One day and multi-day courses, private and custom designed courses are available to fit everyone's schedules, goals, skills, and ages.

191 **The Boathouse Creative Studio** on 381 Main Street (behind Tuff City Radio). Claire Watson Illustration + Design and Tofino Soap Company join forces. Come and see what they are up to!

192 **Check out local photography by Jeremy Koreski.** Pick up a copy of his newly released book *This is Nowhere,* a beautiful compilation of his life work. Inspiration for future photo expeditions and bringing the wild west home with you. You can find it at *Caravan Beach Shop, Kuma,* and many other shops around town.

193 **Visit Kyler Vos' Studio** off Campbell Street, right beside the Tofino Coffee Co. as you come into town. His photography showcases the West Coast outdoors, nature, and surfing.

194 **Jim Swartz's Studio** next to the *Tofino Brew Co.* features carvings, gem stone jewelry. Jim's been here since the '70s and has got some great stories!

195 **Ceramic Artist Daniela Petosa** is known for her modern ceramic tile designs. She does custom work and offers classes. Her work is featured in local restaurants, resorts, and public lobbies. She has a private studio in Tofino.

196 **See Sol Maya's beautiful hand blown glass** pieces

at *SoBo*, *RedCan Gourmet*, the *Wickaninnish*, and *Sacred Stone Spa*. Take home one or a few of his glass sea star pieces as a magical Tofino souvenir.

197 **Visit Henry Nolla's Carving Shed** on North Chesterman Beach right next to the Wickaninnish Inn. The late legendary carver Henry Nolla built the shed where he lived on McDiarmid's land. He helped to build the McDiarmid Cabin on the point and carved much of the woodwork at the inn in return for keeping his little house and workspace on the property. Local carver Feather George Yearsley, was one of the apprentices who worked alongside Nola. Many carvers have come and gone from the space throughout the years, but George remains, where he's known for his carved eagle feathers. Many claim that Henry's spirit remains. Locals call the area Henry's Corner.

198 **The Wickaninnish Inn Gift Gallery** local carvings, jewellery, paintings, prints, and gifts. Their giftshop/ gallery is at the main entrance, but I recommend popping into their *Driftwood Café* to view more artwork on display.

199 **Go see Pete Clarkson's sculptures!** I'm a big fan of his work. Pete has been creating sculptures out of marine debris since he moved to Tofino to work for Pacific Rim National Park Reserve 17 years ago. There's a few on display at *Jamie's Rainforest Inn.* or contact Pete at peteclarkson1@gmail.com for a gallery tour. www.peteclarkson.com

Tofino Shopping

Shop until you drop! Tofino has everything! Tofitians can stay in Tofino for months, even years, without having to leave. From local hand-knit sweaters and slippers, handcrafted jewellery, gourmet delights, outdoor gear, to local caught seafood. It's a shopaholic's dream come true.

One main reason Tofino is truly unique —notice the absence of familiar retail chain stores. This is all possible due to the efforts of the Tofino Town Council in supporting local sustainable independent businesses. Thank you!

Before I go any further...
Tofino has two liquor stores:

1. **BC Liquor Store** is located behind the **Common Loaf Bake Shop** next to Gary's Kitchen. Open every day (minus holidays) 10AM-7PM most days. **250-725-3722**

2. **Maquinna Liquor Store** is open late and located below the Tofino Coop Grocery. Every day 11AM-11PM. **250-725-3877**

200 **Go on a Surf Shop crawl,** try to catch them all in one day! Start off in town at ***Storm Surf Shop/Pacific Surf School,*** continuing to ***Westside Surf Shop, Surf Sister*** up on the hill, ***Long Beach Surf Shop*** across the street, and to ***Live to Surf*** on your way to the beach. Your task: Ask for a surf report at each shop. Pick-up a locally handmade surfboard leash or dog leash from Nina's Cold Surf Company. Built to last.

201 **Surf Sister.** Find out why Tofino is the surf town where women rule! Ask shop and surf school owner Krissy Montgomery why there are so many chicks that rip in Tofino! One of the very few places in the world you can find a very high percentage of estrogen in the water.

202 **Order a custom made surfboard from local shaper Stefan Aftanis from Aftanis Surfboards** or pickup one of his shapes directly off the rack at many of the local surf shops. Make sure to order very far in advance if you choose the custom option, especially in the summer he is very booked up. His team also does ding-repair.

203 **Need outdoor gear?** Some of the best outdoor clothing shops are ***Stormlight Outfitters, Method Marine Supply, Tofino Fishing*** and ***Trading Co.*** Many of these stores have unique, high end, brand name gear and clothing you can wear at the beach and out to dinner. ***Co-op Family Fashions*** has a great selection as well.

204 **Pina Clothing.** This is a local favorite. All prints are handmade locally, Original artwork by local artists/

owner Angie Roussin. You can customize your own clothes as well. Located on Campbell Street next to Rhino Coffee.

205 Check out our one and only Tofino thrift store: *Castaways Value Store* behind *Tuff Beans/Mermaid Tales* off Campbell Street. Owners Lise and John Wynne are lovely. Here you can check out Lise's handcrafted jewellery, specializing in crystals.

206 Head to the Driftwood Gift Shop for a huge gift knick-knack selection of West Coast gems. Clothing, jewellery, souvenirs, collectables and art. Located next to LA Grocery on the corner across from *Co-op Grocery.*

207 Locally crafted soaps, creams, salts from Sharon Whalen and her Seawench Naturals Soaps. Crafted with care, her lovely soaps are made traditionally with combinations of herbs, seaweeds, and nutrients. They can be found in many shops around town including the *Tofino Pharmasave,* Tofino Pharmacy.

208 Mermaid Tales Bookshop. A small store with only good books. They have an amazing collection of local West Coast books, fiction and non-fiction. Great customer service, they'll help you find the perfect book. At the back, you can find some great selection of good quality educational kids toys, toys you cannot find in Toys"R"Us. **Next door, you can't miss the Tofino Brand Store**, especially if you are searching for fun Tofino branded clothing to wear as a souvenir.

209 **Tofino Public Market on Saturdays.** From May to September, every Saturday from 10AM-2PM at the Tofino Village Green beside the Skate Park. See what the Tofitian Artisans are up to.

210 **Vargas Treasures.** For the artsy folks who love unique treasures and collectables. This wee tiny shop is packed with neat things! Owned and operated by a sweet French gypsy named Sandra Vargas. Her father was a well-known costume designer in Montreal, and she was a magician's assistant.

211 **Tofino has two pharmacies: *Tofino Pharmasave* and *Tofino Pharmacy.*** The Tofino Pharmasave is across from the ***Tofino Co-op Grocery,*** and has a solid crew of ladies who will help you will all your medical needs. They have a great variety of health products as well. Tofino Pharmacy on Campbell St. is not just a pharmacy. They have a very large gift shop, clothes, shoes, books, you name it….and Chummas the best English bulldog in town!

212 **Tofino Sea Kayaking Company.** Tofino Sea Kayaking Company boasts a lovely gift and outdoor goods shop on the waterfront Main Street. They have a great selection of books as well.

213 **Co-op Hardware Store.** Our only hardware store in town, get all your camping gear/equipment, knick knacks, tools here.

214 **Beaches Grocery.** This is the cutest little grocery store on the block. Don't let its size fool you, though; you can find almost everything here. Arrive mid morning for some hot, fresh, home-baked muffins from Jupiter Juice Bakery. Also try their homemade sandwiches made daily. The main grocery store in town is **Co-op Grocery,** there's also **LA Groceries** which has more convenience items, open late.

215 **Green Soul Organics is our largest organic health food store.** Located next to the *Wolf in the Fog.* If you are looking for a specific health ingredient they'll most likely have it. A good selection of homemade local goods as well.

216 **Flowers for that special someone? Crab Apple Floral** provides for more than 200 weddings per year in the Tofino area and also provides fresh flowers to some of the best hotels.

217 **Do you love gardening? Visit OCN Garden Center.** Find out here if there are any gardening events happening around town. Trina, the owner, has a wealth of knowledge, and offers a great selection of gardening goods. 619 Tibbs Place.

218 **Find the perfect gift at Tree House Gift Co.** Marcel, the owner, really enjoys having or sharing something special that reminds him of a time or place, and the Tree House Gift Company has Tofino's best selection of unique West Coast inspired gifts, garments, jewellery, books, pottery, souvenirs, and more that will do just that. Located at the end of Campbell across from *Co-op Grocery.*

219 **Visit Caravan Beach Shop.** Owner Jen has a really good eye for unique useful gift items, trendy, stylish local goods for the outdoor beach loving enthusiast.

220 **Amazing Tans Giftshop located next to Tofino Fishing & Trading on Fourth St.** has a wonderful selection of authentic clothing and local goods.

221 **Habit Clothing** on Campbell St. next to ***Rhino Coffee House*** has a great selection of high end women's clothing. Ladies, if you need a nice dinner outfit with accessories, this is the place.

222 **Tofino DNA Clothing** located on Main St. is a funky little clothing shop. They have local Tofino printed t-shirts, sweaters, unique local jewelry and fused art glass pieces.

Rainy Days & Tofino Winter Attractions

Winter in Tofino is super peaceful; you can take in the power and ruggedness of the wild west coast winter storms, in between calm clear days… I find on the colder days the air is ultra-fresh. All of the colors are electrified on the wet days. You can have the whole entire beach to yourself, whereas in the summer you may share it with hundreds of others. The days are either super stormy or windy wet - great for storm watching - or warmer calm tranquil and misty, or sunny and slightly cooler.

223 **Seek out a hot tub and soak for hours.** This is especially a treat after a nice long winter surf session. Feel free to bring a local bottle of wine or a *Tofino Brewery* growler (refillable glass jug) to join.

224 **On wet/rainy days all of the colors of Tofino** are electrified compared to those sunny bright days. Take a walk and just take notice of all the true colors of Tofino, such as the bright green, shimmery leaves of the salal tree. Those leaves make me joyful every rainy day. The green moss on the old cedars. The colors of the sand, the rocks, the driftwood, etc. Bust out the old camera and play around taking some cool shots…the lighting is perfect!

225 **Ancient Cedar Spa** Watch waves crack over the rocks as you soak your feet in a warm, sensational foot bath while wrapping yourself in a cozy white robe. Afterwards, take a long steam in their rock cave with the thundering sound of the waves in the background. Just make sure to hydrate well before and after the bodily detox.

226 **Try Chocolate Tofino's** homemade **Hot Chocolate Elixir** served hot in shop October through May. It's a steamed blend of rich Belgium dark chocolate and magical ingredients. Bring your own cup for a discount!

227 **Have a chowder tasting competition!** Head over to local restaurants and share a bowl of their homemade seafood chowder. See which restaurant makes the best hot, steamy bowl of creamy, West Coast, seafood goodness. Try *Schooner Restaurant, Wildside Grill, Shelter Restaurant, SoBo, RedCan Gourmet* to name a few.

228 **Be the ultimate cold water waterman/ waterwoman** and find the thickest pair of booties, gloves, and full hooded winter wetsuit. The winter is prime time for surfing in Canada! Tip: Pack a thermos filled with hot water and save it to poor down your wetsuit after a long winter session.

229 **Jump puddles.** Grab your rain boots and hunt for puddles; pretend you're a kid again.

230 **Board games near the fire place** with a bottle of Vancouver Island wine or Tofino Beer.

231 **Come check out our local Trivia Night at the Tofino Brewery.** Watch as locals battle it out to win money prizes beginning in January, once a week, throughout the winter months.

232 **Canucks Games at Shelter Restaurant.** Seek Shelter from the winter storms and grab some $3 Tofino Beers and good eats while watching a Vancouver Canucks game.

233 **Go for a bike ride in the rain** or even suit up at the hotel/ vacation rental and bike to the beach in your wetsuit with a surfboard. This is an excellent way to warmup and it doesn't matter if you get wet!

234 **Storm watch!!!** Tofino is storm watching central in the winter time. Witness Tofino's powerful, thrilling, ocean storms at some of the best beaches in the world. Fan of the Twilight Movies? A few scenes were shot here during storm season, but you need not to worry, no vampires here, only sea monsters!

235 **Witness the Big Blow Hole!** There's a Surge Channel and Blow Hole next to Half Moon Bay. With the proper conditions, big swells during a winter storm, witness large ocean surges shoot up high into the air above the hole in a crazy wild natural spectacle. At the south end of Half Moon Bay, follow a trail that leads you to the rocks that overlook the Blow Hole. BE VERY CAREFUL, there can be rogue waves. Never have your back to the ocean, and keep a good distance from the action. Waves are super powerful, dangerous and quick. You'll need raingear and a nice warm thermos.

236 **Hot Springs.** While the temperatures are colder, this is the best time to enjoy the hot springs! In the summer, it can sometimes be too hot and very crowded. In wintertime, you'll most likely have the entire hot springs to yourself! Locals only go during this time.

237 **Act like a local and hunt down some dry wood and make a beach fire in the rain!** Beach fires are not just for dry sunny days. Cozy up in some rain gear, huddle under umbrellas, or just sport your wetty (wetsuit) while the kids splash around in the nearby tide pools with buckets and toys. You can grab some great rainy weather toys for the kiddies at the local Tofino Pharmacy.

238 As the cooler fall weather descends, the waters become much clearer. **Suit up, find a snorkel mask and flippers and check out what's beneath the surface.**

239 **Rent a movie from LA Grocery in town or stream Netflix and cuddle up on the couch** with a warm blanket, a mug of hot chocolate and Baileys Irish Cream. Winter is the time to kick-back and relax.

Kid's Activities in Tofino
(Contributed by Shawna Roberts)

Shawna Roberts lives in Tofino with her husband and two young daughters. She is the co-founder of **Tofino Nature Kids** and has a passion for getting kids outside... no matter what the weather!

The town of Tofino offers many kid-friendly cafes and restaurants as well as fun shops to explore.

240 **Search for glass balls after a storm** - Cox Bay, Florencia and Wickaninnish Beach

241 **Drop in to Nature Kids** for the day. They offer nature connection programs for local and visiting children.

242 Attend **Kid's Day during the Pacific Rim Whale Festival** in mid-March.

243 **Get creative with kelp!** How many things can you make out of kelp?

244 Visit the Tofino Botanical Gardens. There are goats, chickens, and a fun trail network leading down to the mudflats.

245 Build fairy houses along the Tonquin Trail. Perhaps you will spot a mermaid swimming off Tonquin Beach!

246 Set up a 'nature table' on the beach. Display your treasures you have found during your visit, then leave them for others to enjoy.

247 Explore the tide pools at North Chesterman's Beach. Check the tide table for a low tide!

248 Try out the twirly slide at the playground on the Village Green.

249 Create a scavenger hunt outside. Or maybe there is a chest of gold hidden in the sand and a treasure map has been found!

250 Build a log shelter on Long Beach or make a mosaic of shells, rocks and other treasures in the sand.

251 Take a big skipping rope to the beach...or use a long piece of kelp to create your own!

How to have FUN in Tofino when you're 60+

Longtime local Tofitian, Camilla Thorogood, volunteer, master decorator and gardener, provides us with her tips and tricks on how to have the most fun in Tofino when you're 60 +.

1. Easy local beach access at the end of Hellesen Road next to Ocean Village Resort.

2. Warm in car viewing of beautiful Long Beach at the small northern parking lot of Long Beach (also known as Incinerator Rock parking lot). Make sure to get here early morning, to grab a spot. Fills up quickly in the summer. The family can walk the beach, while the grandparents witness the fabulous ocean view from the warmth of the car.

3. Downtown Main Street was recently re-modeled with wide sidewalk areas and plenty of places to sit and rest.

4. Restaurants with easy access: Long Beach Lodge has an easy accessible elevator to their restaurant, which includes one of the most fabulous ocean beach views in the area. They also have a cozy sitting lounge.

The Wickaninnish Inn has a small easily accessible coffee shop, the Driftwood Café, and the Pointe Restaurant with a stunning panoramic view.

Jamie's Rainforest Inn has easy direct walk in access to their restaurant. They have a great breakfast.

Marina West has easy access, with both a pub and restaurant that overlooks the harbor where fishermen bring in their daily catch.

The Sea Shanty Restaurant also has easy access with harbor and government wharf views where you can see a steady stream of boats and planes.

Sobo Restaurant and Schooner Restaurant, during the summer, has level walk-in access as well.

Tofino Annual Events & Festivals

Visit www.251thingstodo.com/tofinoevents for updated annual events in Tofino.

This Is My Tofino, What's Yours?
(Meet the Real, Local Voices of the Community)

Hello! My name is **Agata Pydzinska,** and I am the local dog walker. I moved to Tofino over ten years ago to surf. I have since discovered and fallen in love with everything else this place has to offer. Nearly all of my interests revolve around being active outdoors, in nature and surrounded by animals. Tofino is like a jackpot of endless entertainment as far as I'm concerned.

What I LOVE about Tofino? Where do you begin in a place like this? Tofino has an incredible sense of community, an abundance of nature and a world class culinary scene.

I am a professional dog walker and love my job. Working with animals is highly gratifying and I love how genuine their enthusiasm is. I get to work for myself and spend all day outside in the forests or beaches surrounded by a pack of happy canines.

If I only had ONE day in Tofino, I would start my day with a run on the beach with my dogs followed by a round of golf or some mushroom picking in the forest. I would then sneak in a quick pint at the brewery before an evening with friends at one of the many amazing restaurants. Beach fire anyone?

Tofino Travelling Paws is certified, insured, and registered home based dog care business. We are flexible, accommodating and personal. Whether it's last minute or long term arrangement, we aim to exceed your expectations and return your dog safe, happy, and tired. Please do not hesitate to contact us anytime via email, phone, or text.

tofinotravellingpaws@hotmail.com
250-726-5005
Visit us on Facebook
We would love to hear from you!

My name's **Alan Churchill.** I'm an active community member who volunteers for environmental causes, including Dogwood, Clayoquot Action and Transition Town. I'm a photographer, DJ, web builder, and bike mechanic with an interest in video production and astrology.

I love Tofino's natural environment, which is very important to me. The fact that Tofino has such a tight-knit community is the thing that holds this town together. The rhythm of the seasons is noticeable, and the skies are clear from light pollution.

I currently host a radio show on Tuff City Radio 90.1 FM on Saturday nights. I have a passion for dance, music, and I want to showcase the awesome people doing positive things for environmental and social justice.

If I had ONE day in Tofino, MY Tofino would be to turn off ALL electronics and leave them at home and spend the day outside from sunrise to sunset. Soak in all the beauty and lessons that nature here has for us.

My radio show is called Beats & Treats and is on every Saturday from 8PM until late. Appointments can be made to speak with me on air through *alan@alchurchill.com.*

~~~~~~

Hi, my name is **Johanna (Anna) Vanderkley**. There were no jobs in Victoria, so I came up here in 1985 and found a job and a place to live the next day. I worked at the old Loft Restaurant, the old **Marina West** before the pub was built and it had only four rooms at the time. I use to rent boats, kill crabs and book people into Jamie's Whaling Charters. After six months, I ended up buying an old boat that I converted into a clothing store and called it the Boatique. It was on the dock for three years.

I met Crazy Ron and fell madly in love with him. We later built and opened **Tough City Sushi Bar and the Inn.**

I love Tofino because it's a small town. I love the summertime when it gets very busy with lots of people from all over the place. I love the views out of my windows, looking at the waters and the mountains every day.

~~~~~~~~~~~~~~~~~~~~~~~~~~~~~~~~~~~~

Hi! My name is **Andy Herridge,** and I've lived in Tofino but currently live in Ucluelet, I am the owner/operator of a surf school here called **Wick'd Surf Camps.** I named it in homage to my favorite beach Wickaninnish Beach, or just 'Wick' as it's known. I grew up in Southern Ontario, but I moved to Tofino/Ukee in 2011 from Whistler where I spent 12 years snowboarding and travelling off to distant spots to surf. Eventually the surf bug took over, and I couldn't travel to surf anymore, and I had to live somewhere I could surf every day. So here I am!

What I love about Tofino, and the whole West Coast for that matter, is that the area around the towns that we live in, that's the area we all love to go explore and be a part of every day. Being in the wilderness and exploring the beauty around us is what it's really all about. The people, the wilderness and our connection to it all, that's the three best things about the area.

I teach surfing, do a radio show and even work a night job serving tables. I do it because I love doing it!

If I only had ONE day in Tofino… well depending on the weather I would either take a plane to the hot springs or go for a kayak out into the inlet, then play a round of golf and finish it off with a sunset surf and bevy or two in town with some friends.

If you wanna chat…surf, golf, bikes and or music, come see me at 1559 Imperial Lane in Ucluelet, B.C. I am here year round and open daily 10 – 4 (if I am not in the water that is). Or get ahold of me when I am not at the shop by calling or texting 250-266-0338, email me if you are not in town at andy.wickdsurfcamps@gmail.com or check out my website for prices and details on surf lessons by visiting **wickedsurfcamps.com**

For social media fun stuff check out my;
Instagram - @wickdsurfcamps
Facebook – facebook.com/wickdsurfcamps
Twitter - @wickdsurfcamps

My name is **Anna McKenzie-Sasges,** and I am the front desk manager at Middle Beach Lodge. I grew up in Nanaimo, and my family began visiting Tofino every summer, starting the summer I was born, as well as many times throughout the year. I learned how to walk here, rode a bike for the first time on MacKenzie Beach, and lost my first tooth while visiting Tofino. In the summer of 2013, I was living in Vancouver and looking for a change. I decided to move to Tofino, taking a (what I thought at the time) temporary housekeeping position. Two and a half years later, I'm still as in love with this place as ever.

I always say that Tofino is what you make it; open your heart to this town and extraordinary things will happen. My favourite things in this town are its natural beauty, the people who choose to lay their roots here, and the food. Oh my God, the food! I have never had a bad meal in Tofino!

Middle Beach Lodge is one of my favourite places to be. We have the best continental breakfast I've ever had at a hotel, and freshly baked cookies in the evening. Our hidden gem, though, is our three-course dinner we serve up to five nights per week. The Lodge has a special way of making visitors feel at home, no matter where home really is.

My perfect day in Tofino would be a Wednesday (I'll explain why in a minute). It would start with a bike ride into town for a Matcha and Rancheros Wrap from **Tuff Beans**. I would then head to the **Tofino Botanical Gardens** and tour around there, ending in **Darwin's Café** to read and drink a mug of fresh mint tea. From there, I would head into the park to walk at Schooner Cove, Florencia Bay, and Combers Beach. On the way back to town, stopping at Grice Bay on nice days, calm days, the reflection on the water is breathtaking. Grice Bay is one of my favourite places—it's incredibly calm. I would then pick up some beers at **Tofino Brewing Co.** and get a pizza or dirty mac'n'cheese from **Red Can Gourmet,** and watch the sunset at Middle Beach. Wednesday nights are Karaoke Night at **Jack's Pub,** and I'm a bit of a karaoke superstar. That would be my perfect Tofino day.

〰〰〰〰〰〰〰〰〰〰〰〰〰〰〰

Hey there, my name is **Ariel Weiser Novak!** (Yes, like the mermaid.) I like to read, hang with my friends, and take short to medium walks on the beach, but not longer than that. I hang out with eight year olds a lot. Some fives, sixes, and a bunch of seven and three quarters too, and maybe a couple nines or tens… I teach kids to shred a guitar like they do green faces, strum a ukulele with Irie island vibes, and some classical keys, Christmas carols nowadays. Got an awesome little buddy at the school, we kick it in the playground (shoutout J sauce), and, well, soccer games need a ref, don't they?

Awesome community of families here, with the loveliest little nuggets, bright, polite, full of life and vigor. Really just super excellent. I'm also especially keen on the momentum towards environmental stewardship that is being built in this town. A plethora of organizations focusing positive energy and action towards various important issues, ranging from salmon farming to waste management to sustainable housing. Clayoquot Biosphere Trust, Clayoquot Action, Friends of Clayoquot Sound, Tofino Young Agrarians, and Tofino Ucluelet Transition Towns to name a few.

During the summer I work for the Tofino Ucluelet Culinary Guild (TUCG), distributing organic produce from across the island and the Okanagan to our end-of-the-road towns. Lastly, a permaculture Tofino organization that I'm really excited about will be launching soon. If you have any questions regarding anything environmental in Tofino, or want to get involved, hit us up at *permaculturetofino@gmail.com*.

~~~~~~

I'm **Bree Eddy**, registered massage therapist and lover of nature. I thought I'd surf twice a day, every day, when I moved here. But I don't. I burst out of bed in the mornings just to get outside and breathe the pure air and run alongside the ebbing waves as they lap the shores of the sandy beaches of Tofino. I don't have to check the wind, the swell, the tide...I just GO. Sometimes I'm lucky and my spirited friend will join me on a whim for a run. We'll chat the whole time and run like gazelles and laugh and figure out life, and it's like we're on another planet. The soft early light and water and sand make us fly down the beach like we're not even moving at all. Sometimes I'll scoop my friend's dog and we'll bound down the beach playing chase while his big-floppy tongued smile melts my heart.

I adore that more people are growing food here in Tofino, that lovely, beautiful from the inside out women have many successful businesses in town and that men stroll the beach with their young families. I love the alpine, the water sports, the climate, the forests, the freedom and the raw beauty here.

What I LOVE about Tofino is:

1. The pure water and air.
2. That magic happens here.
3. The time and space to connect with other humans and animals, plants and creatures alike.

I am in love with massage therapy because it allows me to center my life on holistic health and wellness. Where ever I am and whomever I treat, I focus on the relationship between the structure of the body and the way it functions. Massage supports the body's ability to restore and maintain health by using palpation and manual techniques to influence muscles, joints, nerves, connective tissue and internal organs.

If I had ONE day in Tofino, I would wake up, smile, sit, lay, or put my legs up the wall while I was still in bed and breathe or maybe do a light meditation. Then I'd dress and jaunt to the beach to take in the sunrise. Water on my skin and the first light on my forehead definitely kick-start my day and keep my heart soaring for whatever might happen that day! I imagine a shell, a rock, a piece of drift wood, a dog or a person would catch my eye and then I'd start running the beach and let my legs fly. Maybe Kayu, my doggie-partner in crime, would be with me. The beach is like his doggy Heaven, and he always brings the most infectious energy and appreciation for early morning swims and runs. I'd get home and have the hugest lemon-water hot drink you ever did see, then I'd have a bath, scrub, and body balm spa date at home using all things I've learned from my friends out here. I'd leave the house, ready for anything, smelling and feeling like a million bucks. What would happen then?! A stop at Green Soul for some nourishment and inspiration? A spontaneous date from meeting a friend on the bike path? An impromptu boat trip from a local company to Hotsprings or the Wild Side Trail in Ahousaht? A drum circle? Haha. A steam at the Wick? Breakfast at Jamie's? A stop for one of Tofino's special coffees? A SUP, paddle or a beach walk? Hopefully a warm dinner and some spooning while water crashes and light fades into black so the sky looks like a blanket with a million diamonds strewn upon it at the very end of it all.

Tofino Massage Therapy at 451 Main St., offers a variety of treatments. Call us at **250-266-0669** or peruse availability and even book online at ***www.thebreedom.com.***

~~~~~~

Hey, my name is **Brendan Muehlenberg,** and I'm the owner of **SurfCam.ca** and manager of **Relic Surf Shop.** I also do the beach commentary and am in charge of livestreaming every major local surf contest (Rip Curl Pro Tofino, Queen of the Peak, Tofino Paddle SUP/Surf Invitational).

Born and raised on Sproat Lake, just outside Port Alberni, I always enjoyed my time coming out here since I was a little kid. Now after living out here on the West Coast for over nine years, I don't plan on ever moving away from this little jewel I get to call home. Owning a surf company and managing a surf shop, my life pretty much revolves around surfing and all the stresses that come with it (which isn't much). Growing up only an hour away from here, I know the west coast area pretty well. There's a ton of other things that I love doing out here such as hiking, fishing, foraging, adventuring, camping, partying and enjoying the good company of all my friends.

I love Tofino because of how young and happy the town vibes are. Everybody that lives out here has each other's back and is supportive in anyway possible. I also love how much nature plays a huge role in everyone's way of life out here. Everyone appreciates it out here, where I find that many people in this world have lost that basic connection.

If I only had ONE day in Tofino, my day would consist of the following: Wake up in a fancy resort on the beach and check the surf. Make some coffee from Tofino Coffee Co. Surf all morning, then head to the Coop and make a big breakfast for the boys! Then I'd probably go for a hike somewhere (the Cox Bay point hike is pretty rad with a nice view). Then I'd probably go grab some lunch at **Red Can Gourmet, Wildside Grill, Tacofino, Shelter** or **SOBO** (best places in town). Go check the waves again. If the waves are good, go surf, if not, then I'd head to Tofino Brewery and grab a ton of beer and either head to the beach or adventure somewhere. End of the day I'd either go camp somewhere, or if I'm not down for camping, head to Shelter Restaurant and put out the vibe with da boys! Probably end up at Jacks after a few too many!

Make sure you check out www.surfcam.ca! With local surf reports and live streaming cameras on all the beaches out here, it makes that decision "Where should I surf today" that much easier! We are Canada's ultimate surf website.

Hit me up:

Brendan Muehlenberg
www.surfcam.ca
Instagram: @surfcamcanada @brendinobambino
Phone: **250-522-0727**

Hello all, my name is **Cameron Dennison,** and I came to Tofino 16 years ago for a two-week vacation. I am still here and happier than ever! I have the great privilege of being a part of the community as the radio station manager for **Tuff City Radio 90.1 FM.** I run several businesses in town including Strongheart Painting as well as **Strongheart Productions,** a film and productions company. I have lived in some very amazing and wonderful places in the world, though none as stunning, wild and alive as Tofino.

I love the people. I love living on the edge of the world. I love that it takes effort to get here; you don't just show up in Tofino. You have to make a choice to be and live here. I love that this little town on the edge is an international town. You can hear languages from all over the globe being spoken on a daily basis; you can eat at restaurants that are written up all over the world and famous for their awesomeness, the New York Times and on and on… We are small and we are representative of the world. Dynamic, fit and cultural…

I do what I do because I love people, I love music and I love to tie that all together. I love being a part of this community and attending, supporting and hosting events, I love to bring talented artists, musicians and healers to this community and share them with locals and visitors alike!

If I had ONE day in Tofino, I would walk on the beach with my wife and daughter. Then, when they were tired and ready for bed, I would come into the radio station and play all of the music I love and ramble with the intention of helping people to enjoy their time here, their families and their lives as much as I do.

Join us and the Tofino Community live every day at **Tuffcityradio. rocks.** We would love if you would join us and if and when you come, this is how you can take a piece of Tofino home with you. Forever! You never have to leave with Tuffcity Radio.

My name is **Camilla Thorogood.** I'm a volunteer for a lot of community events. That's because it's needed in a small community, and it's my passion.

I love Tofino because of the community, a place where people look out for each other and one of natural beauty.

I work hard with fundraising for the Pacific Rim Hospice Society: I drive seniors around town, I volunteer with the CARE Network (Coastal Animal Care and Education Network) driving animals out to the SPCA, and I volunteer for Cops for Cancer and the Catholic Church, designing and making a quilt every year that is a big part of their annual fundraiser. My biggest volunteer job is my position as the only official volunteer at the Wickaninnish Inn, where I get to use my creative side decorating for Christmas and being consulted for many other events at the Inn.

If I only had ONE day in Tofino, I'd go to the beach—can't beat the beach. If I was younger, I would climb up Lone Cone; I waited too long.

~~~~~~

Hi I'm **Capt. Josh Temple**. As a professional fisherman I've spent a lifetime guided by the movements of fish and the men and women who endeavor to catch them. From remote coastal communities that dot the rugged BC coast to distant tropical seas that span the equatorial region of the globe, I have enjoyed a career that has taken me to some of the worlds most remarkable places in search of adventure, great fishing, and fun.

Tofino is famous for its 5 star resorts, gourmet local cuisine, and eclectic coastal community rich in the history and flavour of the Pacific Northwest. Miles of pristine surf-rich beaches, towering glacial-capped mountains, and a vast playground of ocean, rivers, and lakes literally teeming with fish offers a stunning array of adventure itineraries. In essence, Tofino is heaven for adventurous souls, and that's why I choose to call Tofino home.

I own and operate **Prime Time Adventures,** an adventure tour company offering both fresh and saltwater fishing, whale watching, and adventure tours to discerning travellers.

My typical day in Tofino starts well before dawn. Usually we are loading equipment into the boat, raft, or helicopter and setting off deep into the heart of Clayoquot Sound to fish, hunt, and adventure. If we have to, we eventually come home. But it's like pulling teeth to get us to leave the wilderness.

Prime Time Adventures warmly welcomes families, corporate groups, and beginners and experts alike. Our mandate is to ensure that each and every person on our tours enjoys a safe and remarkable experience every time.

Capt. Josh Temple
Fishing Operations Manager
Ocean Outfitters
368 Main St - Tofino, BC
www.oceanoutfitters.bc.ca

~~~~~~

I'm **Caroline Woodward**, I am a writer and lighthouse keeper based on Lennard Island at the head of Clayoquot Sound since 2008. Besides writing eight books for adults and children so far, I love gardening, cooking and kayaking in my spare time.

I love Tofino for its great restaurants, stunning natural beauty, lots of interesting and happy people.

I am a relief assistant lightkeeper, which means that I fill in when other keepers take holidays or need urgent medical and dental care or have family emergencies to attend to. So far I've worked on ten different west coast light stations. It is a seven days a week for months on end kind of job, and we contribute weather reports for mariners and aviators and collect weather and other scientific date, as well as assisting citizens in trouble when necessary. I enjoy the work and shift work allows me time to write so it suits me very well.

If I had ONE day in Tofino, I would start with the breakfast sandwich at the **Common Loaf Bake Shop,** a tried and true classic, walk down to **The Roy Vickers Gallery** post cards by Kyler Vos to enjoy the art and the soothing ambience, get my hair cut by Jessica at Salty Dolls, enjoy a deep tissue massage from **Bree at Tofino Massage,** walk on Chesterman Beach and wave at Lennard Lighthouse, grab a bicycle and take the paved bike path out to Beaches Plaza to eat a late lunch at **Wildside Grill** (their halibut burger is five stars), pedal back in to the village to buy some good fiction at **Mermaid Tales Bookshop**, pop down to **House of Himwitsa** to buy First Nations-made baby booties for my friend's first grandchild, have a pick-me-up Americano at Main Street Gallery & Espresso Bar, buy some gorgeous postcards made by Tofino painter Marion Syme to add to the lovely postcards by Kyler Vos, the photographer whose gallery is right beside **Salty Dolls**. Hungry again most likely, I'd have sushi at **Tuff City Sushi** because it is simply the best sushi in the entire province.

My latest book is *Light Years: Memoir of a Modern Lighthouse Keeper* (Harbour Publishing: 2015), which is available at **Mermaid Tales Bookshop** and Main Street Gallery & Espresso Bar as well as Blackberry Cove Market in Ucluelet. Visit www.carolinewoodward.ca for more info! Enjoy your stay!

My name is **Catherine Bruhwiler.** I own and operate *Tofino Paddle Surf.* I grew up in Tofino on the beach, back in the day when no one wanted anything to do with headache of driving so far to the docks and the store from way out at the beach. The road at Chesterman's was gravel, and we didn't go to school. Naked hippies carved down at North on the sunny days and we ran around, back and forth on the beach. Into the water and then into the bath to defrost, all day long. The wetsuits just weren't the same then.

Once a person or two discovered how much fun surfing was and came out to rent their gear, we discovered how keen they were to exchange cash for a few surf tips and so began the rise of the surf school. Underground and laid back as it was, a few 13 year olds figured out how to make some fun dollars on the beach doing what they loved best.

Fast forward 20 years. Tofino is well equipped with as many surf schools as it can handle. I've spent 10 years in Mexico learning from the traveling Hawaiians how much fun it is to surf a paddleboard when the waves are one-foot high and nothing else works. I come back home to Tofino and decide I don't want to compete and start another surf school, but I want to be on the water. I want my kids to be able to come to work with me. I don't want to be standing in really cold water all day teaching beginners to surf. No one in Tofino has really seen a paddleboard and they think I'm crazy. I love that, so I use it as fuel and create a small and humble, but skilled and stoked crew of us to teach paddle boarding and open up the world on the water to as many people as we can.

When you can stand on water and see the sand down on the ocean floor, the fish and seals and dolphins, sunshine sparkling off the ripples, that is pretty cool. When you look up and see the glaciers behind the cedar trees that line the beach and the eagle swooping down for a salmon in the setting sun, you think you are in heaven. When more people can love and appreciate what we have, more of us will care and want to protect our coast and our beautiful planet. We hope to change the world, one paddleboard cruise at a time.

Tofino is my home. I do love a trip here and there, but honestly, if I could never get on a plane again and this is where I had to spend the rest of my days, I would be perfectly stoked. And that's saying a lot, considering I've spent most of my life here. I was one-year-old when my parents came to Tofino, and I've lived other places, enough to know that Tofino has everything I love. Good people, fresh air, loads of waves and lots of space to be yourself.

If I had one day left to live, I would spend it in Tofino. I would run the beach with my hair out so I could feel the wind. I would hike to a vista where I could see as far to the horizon as possible, and I would surf and paddleboard with my friends and family until the moon and stars came out, then spend the evening by a fire on the beach.

If you love the beach, the ocean, the fresh air or even just wish you did, come see us for an adventure. You will not be disappointed. Any time of year, there is always something to do outside and a way to enjoy the world. Email us at *info@tofinopaddlesurf.com* or call 250-244-6399 for your adventure.

~~~~~~~~~~~~~~~~~~~~~~~~~~~~~~~~~~~~

My name is **Cedar James**. I am a fine art landscape photographer showcasing the beautiful views of one of the most magical spots in the world, including Clayoquot Sound and the surrounding areas of the Pacific Rim. In addition to photography and art, I enjoy being in nature, surfing, music, and spending time with friends.

I love Tofino because of the wonderful community spirit, and it is one of the most beautiful places on earth. When you come here, you can feel a sense of mystery and magic about it and I aim to capture it in my work. I love her moods as almost every day she offers something a little different. When you visit, she promises to reach out to you in some way you didn't expect.

If I had ONE day in Tofino, I'd go for a surf then hike out to one of my favorite spots, have a fire and watch the sunset with some great food and friends.

I have beautiful options for prints on my website based on their excellence but I can customize just about anything. I have open editions as well as a no compromise collector's edition for the discerning buyer seeking a true museum archival print. Since I shoot medium format which is in a class of its own for photography, almost all of my photographs can go extra-large while holding fine detail. Discounts available if you wish you decorate your home or office with three or more pieces.

Please visit my website at: www.cedarjames.com or email me at: info@cedarjames.com

~~~~~~

My name is **Cindy Hutchison** and my first step onto the Tofino scene happened in November 2012. I randomly threw my name into the "pot" to help organize the décor for the 16th Annual Clayoquot Oyster Festival and I've never looked back. This opened up my world to a beautiful community that I love very deeply. I am a mother of one and try to help out with many wonderful organizations to the best of my ability along with supporting my partner Rob Renna. I adore seeing people happy and enjoying life and I do my very best to make sure everyone is having a good time!

I will be contributing my third Tofino Lantern Festival – August 2016, a fundraiser for the **Raincoast Education Society**, and helping coordinate my fifth Clayoquot Oyster Festival in November 2016. I am the coordinator for the Tofino Boardwalk, a Tofino Arts Council Project that is growing awareness and support for the arts in Tofino, and am co-ordinator with Leah Austin of the Tofino Community Food Initiative, dispelling the rumour you can't grow veggies in Tofino.

I love the power of connection and see the world around me as one big, beautiful web where we all are one.

You can follow and support the projects I'm working on by liking them on Facebook and following them on Instagram or contact me at **cinds.h@gmail.com** for more information or if you'd like to help out!

Clayoquot Oyster Festival
FB: Clayoquot Oyster Festival
@clayoquotoysters

Tofino Lantern Festival
FB: Raincoast Education Society
@raincoasted

Tofino Boardwalk
FB: Tofino Boardwalk
@tofinoboardwalk

Tofino Community Food Initiative
FB: Tofino Community Food Initiative
@tofinolocalfood

My name's **Crazy Ron**. I run a sushi bar and an inn and I want to make a massage parlor.

I met the love of my life in Tofino...but I'm not saying that - everyone will call me a sissy. I got an image to keep up!

I bought one of the first places at Chesterman's Beach, was the third settler at Chesterman's.

I like Tofino because I like dead end stuff. It's dead end street.

Me and my wife created a **sushi bar** because we were addicted to sushi and there was no sushi bar in Tofino. We collected most of the stuff and made our own hotel and restaurant, which we are pretty proud of because it's not easy creating your own restaurant and hotel and being successful at it. Our sushi is excellent! We've always had Japanese chefs.

If I had ONE day in Tofino, I'd have a culinary experience here. Eat and drink my face off.

I have plans to build a lighthouse, and our aspirations are to open an Italian restaurant. People can reach me by phone, email...or go right to my house next door, girls only though!

~~~~~~

My name is **Daniel (Daan) Delen** and I am part-owner at **Ocean Outfitters.** My passions are living off the grid, which I do on Neilson Island, and the wildlife and nature around here in Tofino and being able to introduce that to customers.

I love Tofino for its rawness and wildness of everything around here, particularly outside of town rather than inside of town.

If I had ONE day in Tofino, I'd do some wildlife viewing, a bit of fishing, and a bit of hiking, but really just being OUT there in the wilderness and enjoying everything that Tofino has to offer.

~~~~~~

My name is **Dan Harrison**. I'm a forest ecologist, fisherman, and the executive director of the **Raincoast Education Society.** I'm passionate about the natural world, the people and the cultures of Clayoquot Sound, and how to live in balance with the natural cycles that define the region.

I love that Tofino is dominated by natural forces, and that a key part of thriving in this part of the world is a deep understanding of how to interact with these elements. Whether it's understanding how the wind and tides will affect your day on the water, or how a particular swell will produce surfable waves at a local beach, you are always rewarded for your knowledge of a place. Such an understanding forces you to realize that you are part of something much larger, and to appreciate and respect the world we inhabit.

The **Raincoast Education Society** is a non-profit organization dedicated to conserving the ecosystems of Clayoquot Sound through education and research. We provide a range of adult and youth education programs, including field courses, workshops and guided tours. Join us to explore the lush rainforests and rich marine ecology of the region!

If I had only ONE day in Tofino, I would rise early and head offshore at sunrise to fish for Chinook salmon. By mid-day, I'd head in for a picnic and a hike through the old-growth rainforest. I would then head to the beach for a sunset surf and round out the day with a big beach dinner of fresh caught salmon cooked over a bonfire with good friends.

Visit us at **www.raincoasteducation.org.**

My name is **Dan Lewis**, and I've been calling Tofino home since 1991. My passion is doing wild things in wild places, especially kayaking. At home I'm working on reading the classics and becoming fluent in the Nuu-chah-nulth language.

I moved here after paddling around Vancouver Island in 1990, because it was obvious this was the Last Great Rainforest on the Island.

In 1993 I helped organize the Clayoquot Summer logging protests, and in 2013 founded Clayoquot Action to help protect this place from risks posed by mining, salmon farming, and pipelines.

Every Tuesday in July and August my partner Bonny and I do a free presentation at the Clayoquot Community Theatre. Check it out—you will be stoked and inspired to keep this place wild! To reach me: email *dan@clayoquotaction.org.*

Cheers,
Dan Lewis
cell 250-726-8136
office 1-877-422-9453

Hi, my name is **Danby Russell White**. I have lived in Tofino most of my life and have always been into artwork. All throughout high school, art class was the only thing I looked forward to. After a few years in my early 20s not doing any artwork I got a tattoo that I actually drew for myself. I think this woke me up a little and made me realize I needed to get back into art in a meaningful way. That was 2009, when I got into doing tattoos. I also love doing surfboard art work as well; its usually an interesting shape and instead of looking at a square/rectangle white canvas you design something for that particular board. It's a lot of fun!

Tofino to me has its ups and downs, just like anything and everywhere. For people who live in Tofino, leaving for even a small amount of time shows you just how special it is here and how lucky we are. The grass can be pretty green here.

I would say I do tattoos, water colours, surfboard art and T-shirt designs for the most part. I call my studio and a few friends **Tuff City Pricks**.

If I had ONE day in Tofino, I'll try to be honest with this one, I would have to say wake up early and either go for a surf or to the hot springs on a friend's boat. Get back to town and go for breakfast at the **Common Loaf Bake Shop**. Do a tattoo on a good friend, then go build a huge fire at the beach and light some fire works. I would say that would be a nice time.

Check out my FB page: www.facebook.com/danbyrussell Instagram: @TCPART

~~~~~~~~~~~~~~~~~~~~~~~~~~~~~~

My name is **Daniel Lamarche**. I was born and raised in northern Quebec. I first visited Tofino Long Beach in 1969. I was then 17, travelled through North-South America and Europe. Tofino was drawing me back time after time until I decided to make this place my home. I have been a full time resident since 1972 when I purchased a piece of land and build my home.

I own and operate with my wife Barbara **Tofino Cedar Furniture LTD** (formerly Clayoquot Crafts) established in 1993. Our motto always was Made in Tofino by locals from local wood. We started selling to several of the exclusive resorts in the area. Soon, private customers and smaller businesses, including bed and breakfasts, were purchasing our products for their homes and businesses. Over the years, we re-designed our products so that visitors could take a Tofino souvenir home with them. Today, we ship our fine cedar furniture around the world. As our business grew in popularity, we outgrew our home base. So, in 2007, we moved our operations just down the road to an industrial area close to "downtown" Tofino. The larger shop and shipping area means we can better serve our customers, wherever they live.

I love Tofino because of its lifestyle and beauty. I love that my children were born and raised in Tofino. I met my wife Barbara here over 30 years ago who visited Tofino for the same reason and never left.

If I had only ONE day in Tofino, I'd go for a hike in the woods, and have dinner and a Cedar Sour at Wolf in the Fog.

Daniel and Barbara Lamarche
Tofino Cedar Furniture LTD
671 Industrial Way
www.tofinocedarfurniture.com
250-725-3990

~~~~~~

Hi, I'm **Darcy Boulton**, a 35-year-old Tofitian with a passion for projecting, camping, boating and winter touring. I feel pretty lucky to be here in Tofino and to be surrounded by friends and family, pets and possibilities!

When arriving to the small harbour side community of Tofino, you've got Kennedy Lake behind you, sandy beaches to the left and inlets and islands on the right. We are surrounded by rich forests, fishy creeks, mountains and ALL THIS bodes well with me!

I build houses and blend spices (and I do this because I get to do it) with my two bros, Doug and Fraser. We are "Boulton Bros Contruction" and "Boulton Spice All Purpose Seasoning."

If I had ONE day in Tofino, I'd like my day to include an early morning stroll with my lady and out up to Cox Mt., followed by a quick dip and then brunch and a Caesar. Then I'd like to get out on the water, to do a little crabbing and scallop diving. Assuming that I'm not allowed to wake up in Tuff tomorrow, I suppose I would then head up to Hot Springs Cove for an evening cook, camp and soak! Thanks Tofino!

~~~~~~~~~~~~~~~~~~~~~~~~~~~~~~~~~~~~~

Hey Fish & Chip Lovers! This is **Debbie McCartney**. I have lived in Tofino for 44 years and have raised four boys here. I have worked in restaurants since I was 15.

I love Tofino when it is busy and hope you love Tofino as much as the locals do.

If you like fish, burgers, chowders, and tacos call Big Daddy's Fish Fry for hours and delivery 250-725-4415, or visit us at 411 Campbell Street. Open everyday from Spring Break to Thanksgiving.

~~~~~~~~~~~~~~~~~~~~~~~~~~~~~~~~~~~~~

My name is **Dede Monette**, founder and operator of Tofino Yoga.

I landed in Tofino in 2002, after a wonderful journey half way across the world. As you can imagine, I instantly fell in love with Tofino! This is where I met my husband, where I raise my children, where I became intimately connected with everything relating to the ocean and where I traded my skis for my beloved wooden surfboard, which I still ride today!

Tofino Yoga is a happy marriage between outdoor adventure and anything relating to yoga: beach yoga, SUP yoga, yoga retreats, bridal yoga & kids' summer camps.

I love Tofino because Tofino treats me well! Everyday I get to be immersed in nature, either surfing or walking the beaches. I feel nourished, healthy and alive from it all, and ultimately, this is what I wish to share with every Tofino Yoga guest.

If I only had ONE day in Tofino, I would most definitely jump in the ocean. Yes, that's right! Either surfing, SUP'ing or swimming.

Tofino Yoga's most popular offering is our **Tofino Yoga Custom Retreat,** which allows you to book a retreat package, at your own convenience, stay at your preferred accommodation and experience a yoga retreat, all within your own schedule. We happily offer discounted rates to larger groups.

Additionally, we cater to Beach Yoga, SUP Yoga, Private Yoga, Bridal Yoga and Kids Yoga.

Please visit our website to familiarize yourself with all our offerings and services and conveniently sign-up for our monthly newsletter.

Thank you kindly,

Namaste

Dede Monette, Founder & Operator of Tofino Yoga

www.tofinoyoga.com

info@tofinoyoga.com

250-266-2224

My name is **Dom Domic**. I am the President of the Canadian Surfing Association (CSA), which is the recognized national governing body for competitive surfing by the Canadian Olympic Committee and the International Surfing Association. I have been organizing surf contests in Tofino since 1988, and with a very probable inclusion in the Toyko Olympics in 2020, Tofino will play host for the Canadian Olympic and PanAm qualifiers! I'm very excited that there may be some Tofitian Olympians.

As a surfer, Tofino's draw for me is obvious. This town is very unique due its accessibility to surfable beaches and its open exposure to the Pacific Ocean; no other town has that combination on the west coast of Canada. This combination is not only great for surfing, but the coastline is incredibly raw and the landscape is spectacular. There is something amazing that happens to the human soul when one first sees the Pacific Ocean from the end of the road, and that magic stays with you for a lifetime.

I feel like I've done quite a few things but no other activity makes me feel as connected and given me such pure bliss as surfing. I wish I could explain what it is about riding waves that brings that much happiness, but I don't have the words.

In Tofino there is so much to do, see and experience, but for me, if I had only a day, I would just find a beach with a fun wave and surf.

Check out Canadian Surfing Association page on Facebook or go to **www.csasurf.org** and come to the CSA National Championships on the last weekend of May.

My name is **Don Travers,** and I am a mariner who settled in Tofino in 1989 after having travelled around the world and sailed several oceans. I have owned and operated **Remote Passages Marine Excursions** on the Tofino waterfront for over 20 years, offering memorable marine experiences to travelers visiting our area.

Tofino seems to have what everyone is looking for. It's about the geography, the people and the rich cultural and natural history of the area. Tofino sits between the ocean and the wilderness. When you live in Tofino you are balancing on the edge.

Operating our tour company, **Remote Passages Marine Excursions,** allows us – myself, my wife Kati, and our crew -- to connect people to the ancient rainforest, the ocean, and the wildlife. We believe that "Connection is protection," and work with this in mind every day we are hosting guests on the water.

If I had ONE day in Tofino, I would grab my camera and head out on the water. If the tide was low in the early morning, I'd go looking for bears -- between the angle of the morning light and the abundance wildlife in the intertidal, there would be good opportunities for some of those National Geographic photo moments. Then I would head my boat out towards the outside coast in search of whales and sea otters. Even without these sightings, the outside coast islands are a fantastic place to explore.

Please come down to the **Remote Passages Marine Excursions'** base – our authentic waterfront base on Wharf Street. Take photos from the viewpoint at the end of our dock, enjoy a cup of complimentary tea, and check in with the crew at 'Remote' to plan your day (or week) of exploration, adventure and inspiration in Tofino and Clayoquot Sound. Visit our website at **www.remotepassages.com**, or call us at 250-725-3330.

Hi, my name is **Doug Boulton**. I am a local adventure seeker and long time resident of Tofino. I surf, fish, hike, splitboard and beachwalk as much as I can! As a young outdoor enthusiast, Tofino offers it all. I am active in a lot of volunteer events throughout town and am always amazed at the community involvement as a whole.

I love that Tofino is a small outpost at the edge of a marine mountain wilderness, the love and strength throughout the community, and the influx of happy adventurous people, gets me to keep exploring deeper into our surroundings.

I am co-owner/lead carpenter with Boulton Bros Construction along with my two brothers. (Twelve years and rolling). We are builders by nature and continue it into the evenings on various projects. We are also launching a family spice/seasoning company as we feel our tasty product needs to be shared. Boulton Spice is an all purpose seasoning designed for meat, eggs, potatoes, veggies and just about anything, great for BBQ/camping, dining, meals on the go.

If I had ONE day in Tofino, I'd wake up to a surf check/ beachwalk. Proceed to have a homemade breaky. Hit the water for a mid-day salmon troll for coho, then crab. Back in time for evening surf. Beers and dinner with friends to finish the day off.

~~~~~~

My name's **Drew Burke,** and I'm the owner of Tofino Travel Company, which offers all-inclusive surf camps out here on the West Coast. I grew up on Vancouver Island and was drawn to this amazing corner of the earth because I love forests and beaches and wanted to be in the surf all the time. I'm very lucky to be able to call Tofino my home and to live in an environment that inspires me each and every day. With our surf camps I get to share that with other people and they get to sink into the lifestyle here for a week. In that way they end up living and breathing what it's like to live in Tofino; to wake up each morning and head down to the beach.

Obviously our camps are all about jumping in the ocean and going surfing every day, but we go on hikes in the National Park and on a tour around town. My favourite part of the Tofino tour is pointing across the harbour to the Tla-o-qui-aht village of Opitsaht and telling them that it's been inhabited for at least 5,000 years and that Clayoquot Sound is the anglicized word for Tla-o-qui-aht Sound. Many visitors have heard about the protests surrounding the clear-cut logging that happened here in the 1980s and 1990s, but what they may not know is that if it wasn't for the actions of the Tla-o-qui-aht and other First Nations, this area would have been completely destroyed.

One of the most important teachings I've learned from the Tla-o-qui-aht is to leave the land better than we found it. Taking that to heart, we have started a program with Central Westcoast Forest Society where we plant a tree for each day a guest stays at one of our camps. These trees are planted in newly protected riparian areas along salmon-bearing creeks and streams that have been damaged by logging, so they'll literally grow for hundreds and hundreds of years. In this way our surf camp guests not only have the time of their lives in the ocean, but they also get to be part of making Tofino even better than it was when they arrived.

The Original Tofino Travel Company (Consumer Protection BC Travel Agency Licence #65692)

www.tofinotravel.com
info@tofinotravel.com
250-725-2202

1-844-725-2202
Instagram: tofinotravel
Facebook: Tofino Travel

~~~~~~

Hi, my name is **Eugene Tom** and people in Tuff call me **SKIIS**. I was born and raised in Opitsaht (across the inlet from the town of Tofino).

I've been working in the Tofino tourism industry since 1989, and have met many people from all over the world. I've worked in many fields: cook, busser, host, waiter, night cleaner, maintenance worker, and bartender.

For the last five seasons, I've worked at Clayoquot Wilderness Resort as a tour guide. Occasionally I'll drive my cousins water taxi, Miss Daniell.

If I had ONE day in Tofino, I'd recommend going to see Meares Island Trail, Lonecone and a day trip to Cannery Bay. If you can go river fishing do it! There's lotsa trout out there.

Enjoy our small town of Tofino and the scenery. Just giv'r and get out there! Sincerely, Eugene (Skiis) Tom.

~~~~~~

My name is **George Patterson**. I have lived in Tofino for 25 years. The town had a population of 800 when I arrived. We now have about 2,000 people living here. I like it better now, and look forward to 5,000 residents.

Life in Tofino encompasses all of the miseries and joys of life in any other place. The natural world around us assuages the grief and waters the happiness.

Tofino Botanical Gardens is a personal project that is becoming a public place. The garden is not the new, the fast or the exciting. It is just a quiet place where people can come, slow down, and set their hearts free.

If I had ONE day in Tofino, I'd go for a walk on Chesterman's Beach, eat some oysters for lunch, and finish the day at the gardens, watching the tide come in and then go out. Or, maybe, I would go puddle boarding.

The garden is not a terrific product with a great brand. It is a real place that must be experienced in real time. We invite you, your family and friends to witness the intricate place between culture and nature. We are located at 1084 Pacific Rim Hwy, Tofino, BC. Ph: (250) 725-1220.

~~~~~~

Hi, my name is **George Smith** and I'm one of the local pharmacists, and the very first pharmacist in Tofino. I am a business person. I love selling anything, finding anything, and travelling the world.

I love Tofino for its tourists, and talking with them about the world. I love the locals for their special needs, strange requests, for obscure things. I love the nature, ocean, and beaches. I love Chummus the bulldog.

I do what I do because there's a need for a pharmacist. I love to find things that people want, or didn't know that they want.

If I had ONE day in Tofino, I'd visit Chummus at the Pharmacy, and bring your own balloon.

My name is **George Yearsley**, and I've been a wood carver at Henry Nola's carving shed off and on for 15 years. I'm passionate about the wood I use. The ancient old growth wood, the history that lies within those fibers, all the lives that animals and birds have experienced, the storms, and all of the life force those trees have experienced are all in that tree, and so when you approach wood that is 500 years old and older, there's a lot of history there that you have got in your hands. You need to be mindful and respectful to how you approach using it and bring out the best you can in yourself to use that wood. There's nothing worse when you are carving something that old and it doesn't turn out, because then you feel you have not honored the wood to the level it needs to be honored.

What I love about this place are the old growth forests and the wilderness. I need to be around them, and I need them very close to me. Henry was the ultimate driving force that brought me here. I used to come here for years doing kayak and backpacking trips with friends, and then I met Henry. Watching him carve on the beach, I thought, Wow, I'd like to do this. I asked if I could hang out and learn, and he said sure.

The biggest lesson that Henry taught me, indirectly and without any of his intention—because it was who he was—that what he was doing, this was what I wanted to do with my life.

If I had ONE day in Tofino, I would be torn since I don't drive. I would take my dog out to Schooner Cove and hike the beach all day, but otherwise, I'd go to the inlet, away from the surf and the noise, accessible via Sharp Road or the Botanical Gardens. Here, you can look across to Meares Island, which is wild. You know there's an intact salmon stream right across from you, there are wolf tracks along the mudflats, and you are immersed in an old growth forest. You can get in touch with yourself in this space of calm and quiet.

Hi, my name is **Gisele Maria Martin.** I am a citizen of Tla-o-qui-aht First Nation, whose territory the town of Tofino is located in.

I work in cultural education and am a lifelong apprentice. Many individuals from my extended family and First Nation communities have contributed to my learning. The living lands and waterways of our ancestors are my biggest teachers.

The protection of our home, it's spirit and all the species that belong here are of really high importance to me. I've worked and volunteered as an advocate for Tla-o-qui-aht Tribal Park and for the revitalization of our endangered language, Nuu-chah-nulth. The world view expressed in our ancestral language is key to a meaningful relationship with this place.

If I had only ONE day in my home, I would go out and listen. I would visit with the ravens, smell the sand & forest plants and eat from our ancestral gardens. I would spend time with my nieces and nephews because it makes me really happy to witness them growing up rooted in this land, the foundation of our Nation and cultural identity.

The Tla-o-qui-aht Tribal Park declaration is vital in helping to protect this place, and is part of ensuring that our culture continues to survive.

Many people come to visit this beautiful place year round now, and though tourism seems more sustainable than destructive industrial forestry, mining, or aqua-culture fish farming, it still can make a big impact. Traditional teachings such as 'iisaak', respect for all life, may help to guide visitors and newcomers in touring with less negative impact to the lands, waters and life forms of this place.

www.tla-o-qui-aht.org

Hi, my name is **Glen Kaleka** and I am the owner of **Tofino Bike Co.** We offer Bike Rentals in Tofino, BC. We are located near the beaches in the same complex as Tacofino and Live to Surf. We are passionate about getting people out of their cars and into nature, and a bicycle rental is the perfect way to do it!

I love Tofino for the wilderness, the wildlife, and the type of person that the environment attracts. Tofino is not easy to get to, and therefore the people that come understand that some of the best things in life are not always easy to find!

Tofino Bike Co has a fleet of 40+ new bikes available for rent, short term or long term with different styles to suit your preference. We are easy to find and right next to Tacofino and Chocolate Tofino! We offer delivery service and can help you plan your bike adventure with knowledge about the best places to visit on two wheels.

If I had ONE day in Tofino, I'd bike! Our favorite tour starts at our location between Chesterman Beach and Mackenzie Beach and travels South towards the Pacific Rim National Park. Exploring Cox Bay, Sunset Point, Rosie Bay and Chesterman Beach before taking the Municipal Bike Path to Tofino. Once in Tofino there are many great shops and eateries to visit without having to worry about a parking space for your car! Being on a bike in Tofino is the absolute best way to see your surroundings!

We offer discounts on long term rentals and can work with any group needs to customize a package. We rent beach cruisers, commuters, mountain bikes, kids' bikes, chariots, baby seats, and surfboard racks. We also are able to do basic repairs and sell parts and accessories.

Please find us at **www.Tofinobike.com** for all your bike needs in Tofino. We are located at 1180 Pacific Rim Highway next to Tacofino. We are open seasonally from May to October - 10 am - 5 pm daily.

My name is **Godfrey Stephens,** I came to Wreck Bay (now known as Florencia Bay) in 1968, a beautiful amphitheater in the universe!

Carving, painting, and drawing with endless inspiration. I've built wooden boats, a 30 FT Ketch using driftwood, flotsam/jetsam, and locally milled planks. There was much wood on the beaches in the early days before the logging. One of my logger friends says "Oh Godfrey, you are not very cosmic, it will all be back in 10,000 years!"

When we got kicked off Wreck Bay in the early 70's, I built a homemade teepee above the old Wickaninnish Inn, then party capital of the world, on Long Beach. Carving many sculptures, there I met great friend Henry Nola.

Parks Canada bought one of my Red Cedar Abstract sculptures in 1971 for Princess Anne when she opened Pacific Rim National Park at Green Point. With that money, I bought a new Klepper Sailing Kayak, the start of a sailing life. Sold that kayak and built a 36 FT Wharram catamaran, which I promptly sailed around Vancouver Island not knowing much about nautical cruising. That was 1972, then 32 years old. I gradually learned the ropes and decided never to stop rocking. Now 76, I'm still doing it! My daughter Tilikum was born aboard at the 4th street dock in Tofino, 40 years ago!

In 1984, a lot of people were absolutely infuriated that Meares Island was slated for clear cut logging; it would all be bald if it wasn't for a lot of people uprising. Joe Martin and his father knew where this wind fallen 300 year old Red Cedar tree was on Meares Island. Joe cut a 16 FT piece, dragged it out of the woods to Strawberry Island, and two weeks later the roughed out Weeping Cedar Woman was carved in time for the First Great

International Protest and blockade to save Meares Island. You can see the restored Weeping Cedar Woman standing in Tofino's Village Green.

I love Tofino for the interaction with the Indigenous people. Their humor is beyond; they can outdo anybody. I absolutely love the native culture and history. The first contact history, it's just so crazy wild. There's evidence of it still on the beaches. I've found taffrails of old ships. Corners of bays were deep in ancient logs, flotsam and jetsam from all over the world! My great friend/builder/original surfer (Bruce 'Bruno' Atkey) once found 95 Japanese glass fishing floats.

If I had ONE day in Tofino, in the old days I'd go to the Maquinna Pub and have fun with all of my friends. Nowadays it's *Jack's Pub*. I'd recommend getting out on the water, the Sound is huge, and there's so much to see!

~~~~~~~~~~~~~~~~~~~~~~~~~~~~~~~~

Hi, we are **Gord and Leah Austin,** and we own and operate **Tofino Cake Studio**. Gord is a pastry chef, and Leah is a master gardener who grows the edible flowers that decorate Tofino Cake Studio's cakes and cupcakes. Gord has worked with Chef Matthias Conradi and others at the world-renowned Wickaninnish Inn. Leah used to manage the Ancient Cedars Spa at the Wickaninnish Inn for several years before going into business with Gord and creating Chocolate Tofino in 2003, developing it into a successful business before passing the torch to current owners Kim and Cam Shaw in 2010. Gord was the master behind many recipes for chocolate truffles and ice cream that are still enjoyed today.

We now have a local bakery called **Tofino Cake Studio** that specializes in cakes and cupcakes to order that are made with natural, organic and local ingredients. Our mission is to "make people happy with good food." We hand-craft all of our creations with love in a commercial kitchen built into our home that allows us to be close to our young daughter.

We are committed to sustainable practices, from using organic and local ingredients to a reduced footprint (green initiatives include using solar hot water, using FSC paper products, delivering in a hybrid vehicle, and supporting local farmers).

Tofino Cake Studio can easily accommodate special dietary needs such as allergies or gluten-free and vegan diets.

Reach us at 250-725-2594

www.Tofinocakestudio.com

Hello, I'm **Hanna Scott**. I've been living in Tofino for six years. I originally moved here from Victoria so I could be as close to the surf as possible and therefore be in the water as much as possible…As time goes on I'm continuously becoming more in love with this place and always finding another new watery nook to explore.

If I had ONE day in Tofino, I think I would do what I do most days anyway. Wake up, head across the street for a look at the surf but really I'm already in my suit because who checks the surf anyway? Have a million party waves with all the home skillets. Go home make two hard boilers. Eat said hard boiled eggs on the bike ride to the skatepark (I peeled 'em at home). Roll around a little while and hopefully learn something from all the ridiculously shredding micro groms. Winds dying down, head home, pop into **Storm** and **Surf Sister** to say hello to the crews! Go for another surf just because and visit all the kind dogs wandering ownerless on the beach. Catch a crab floating in the ocean and give it to a friend passing by. Bike back into town and meet all the hungry hippos at **Tuff City Sushi** for a feast!

~~~~~~~~~~~~~~~~~~~~~~~~~~~~~~~~~~~~~~

My name is **Jaesn Singer,** and I am a shopkeeper at Beaches Grocery. I've lived in Tofino for six years. I came here when I was a teenager; fell in love with the place, and knew for certain that one day I'd call it home.

Three reasons I will never leave Tofino: One, I love the people. They are a friendly, generous, and creative lot. Also they acknowledge one another rather than ignore each other, and I love them for it. Two, Nature. I mean, seriously, this place is full on magical, and all I have to do is step outside my home to experience it. Three, as much as I love this supernatural wilderness, I am something of an indoor cat. And for me, there is nothing like being inside a warm, comfortable environment and listening to the rain suddenly increase in volume so fast that I can't help but to stop and be in the moment.

If I had ONE day in Tofino, I'd get up "early". Go to **Wildside Grill** for a Breakfast Chibata. Eat it there. Go to Beaches Grocery to pick up a mid-day snack. Head down to Radar Beach and spend the early afternoon exploring the shore. Back to town for a light lunch and margaritas at **SOBO**. Then to Chesterman Beach to play bocce ball till sunset. Campfire salmon for dinner. Then relax in front of the fire, talking and listening to the waves crash to shore.

~~~~~~~~~~~~~~~~~~~~~~~~~~~~~~~~~~~~~~

Hi, I'm **Jaime Ivars Hewitt**, general manager at Tofino Fishing. I moved to Tofino on a gut feeling three years ago chasing waves and the calm, nature immersed lifestyle that is Tofino. It was love at first sight, and I haven't looked back ever since!

I love how abundant this place is; you can fish and forage for all your food quite easily. The waves are consistent and the people are some of the friendliest you will meet.

I run **Tofino Fishing and Jay's Fly & Tackle Shop.** I love fishing, and the waters around Clayoquot Sound offer some world class salmon and halibut fishing. Let us take you out for a memorable time on a private or shared charter. Or come check out our shop to get some local knowledge on the best fishing spots and what lures are working at the moment.

If I had ONE day in Tofino, I would wake up early, grab a coffee at Tofino Coffee, hop on my boat and go after some salmon. After, I would grab a quick bite at **Rhino** around lunch time and head for a surf, and if the waves were small, I would head over to one of the secret honey holes and do some spearfishing. Afterwards, I would come home and prepare the day's catch on the BBQ with some friends and some cold ones from the brewery.

Come say hi at Jays Fly and Tackle Shop (Tofino Fishing), to book a personal fishing experience, where you can have me as your guide. Or check out all we have to offer at the store, buy or rent top of the line fishing gear, clothing, custom made lures, and everything you need to take up spearfishing.

Jay's Fly & Tackle Shop (Tofino Fishing)
561 Campbell St, Tofino BC
We are open seven days a week from 9 am to 6 pm
250-726-4115
www.Tofinofishing.com

Hi, my name is **Janice Wong** and I've been living on the West Coast for the past 10 years and am happy to call Tofino my home sweet home. I moved to the West Coast after falling in love with surfing in my first year UBC and relocated permanently after completing a Geography Major. A nature enthusiast, I love anything and everything to do with being in and on the ocean, whether it's surfing, diving, or taking a joy ride out to explore Vargas. I am passionate about travelling and exploring all that Tofino and the Clayoquot Sound has to offer, which includes sharing my love for this area, the nature and wild life with others via tours with Jamie's Whaling Station and Adventure Centres.

I love Tofino because of it's raw beauty. This place is amazing for 1) beautiful pristine beaches and clean waves, 2) mind blowing sunsets, and 3) epic trails to hidden views. Not to mention all the beautiful people that live here that build a strong community of caring and support. I think simplicity is a key to happiness, and I love how Tofino offers just that, a simple way of living. It's easy to wake up everyday to smell the roses and watch the salty sea outside your window.

I work for **Jamie's Whaling Station and Adventure Centres** because it's an outlet to the ocean and a way of seeing all that this area has to offer. Jamie's experienced, guided marine tours offer guaranteed wild life sightings, Hot Springs Cove adventures, and can link you up with kayaking and hiking to get you to know the West Coast. You can have breath taking encounters and see some of the most amazing things out on the water.

ONE day in Tofino is never enough, but one day of activities could include waking up, grabbing a chai latte and a buddy to head to the beach for an early surf. Returning home to pack lunches and 4x4'ing out to Virgin Falls to have a picnic by the waterfall. Returning home for a late afternoon boat trip to dive for scallops or check the crab trap, which would hopefully yield dinner for the night. Home cooked meals while watching the evening sunset with friends are the best!

If you would like to go explore come down to **Jamie's Whaling Station and Adventure Centres** at 606 Campbell St. across from **Shelter restaurant.** We are open every day from March to November, or call 250-725-3919 to book a tour!

~~~~~~

Hey, **Jan Janzen** here, a.k.a. Jan the man, visitor since 1967, resident since 1987. I came for a two-month sabbatical from Vancouver life and never left!

I feel Tofino as a tiny human enclave in the immensity of Clayoquot Sound: nature so powerful, so beautiful. That energy permeates, informs and inspires all who are open to it.

I create "structural art" using gorgeous driftwood, split boards and lumber (milled by Ben & Nick from salvaged logs). See examples of my work around town or look in "Builders of the Pacific Coast" (pp. 126-139 Shelter Publications). I've written one book (so far) called "Rumours", poetic prose reportage of metaphysical/ worldly experiences. Find it at the library or local book sellers. I also volunteer with Pacific Rim Hospice Society, since 2001.

If I had ONE day in Tofino, I would wake up without an alarm clock, have a leisurely morning with my beloved wife Thérèse, do some creative work, walk or ride my bike on the beach, socialize with fabulous locals (and perhaps some interesting visitors), eat delicious food from our high quality eateries, relax, gratefully take in the beauty of it all, then lie down to sleep, listening to the surf, maybe some rain, and the peace and quiet of a day well spent.

"Rumours", poetic prose reportage of metaphysical/ worldly experiences. Find it at the library or local book sellers. I also volunteer with Pacific Rim Hospice Society, since 2001.

～～～～～～～～～～～～～～～～～

Hi, my name is **Jean-Paul Froment**. I am a second generation Tofino resident that grew up on Chesterman Beach. I am also a husband, a father of two children, and one of the owners of **Live To Surf – The Original Tofino Surf Shop,** our family business since 1984.

After having been to many beautiful areas of the world, I still choose Tofino to be my home.

I love Tofino because it's remote, yet still very connected; easily accessible, yet removed. Steps in almost any direction will take you into the wilderness. We are surrounded by mountains and ocean, epic food, eclectic culture and year-round consistent surf.

I surf and enjoy the outdoors as much as I can, and love that my job allows others to do the same!

If I only had ONE day to enjoy Tofino, I would play on the beach with my kids, surf, eat fresh seafood and exhaust myself outdoors.

If you want get in the water and have fun, come visit us at Live To Surf. We offer Sales, Rentals, and Lessons for everyone!

www.Livestosurf.com
(250) 725-4464
1180 Pacific Rim Hwy, Tofino

I'm surfing junkie **Jeff Beattie**. I surf a lot and work a little. I'm passionate about making good surfing memories.

Besides surfing, my favorite thing about Tofino are the mild winters. I love also how it's populated with mostly fit, artistic, happy people. I love being off the beaten path in a small beach town with a nice community feel.

I do all types of work to stay busy in the winter, but in the summer I'm a surf instructor. I'm stoked when I see people popping up for the first time, and especially the kids, seeing the local groms progressing and getting good is great!

If I had only ONE day in Tofino, I would do the same thing I do every day. Go for a run on the beach in the morning to check the surf, maybe hook up with a friend for a surf and eat a lot of fresh seafood.

~~~~~~

My name is **Jerry Cloutier**. I served for 20 years in the Canadian Military and currently work at the Tofino Co-op Gas Bar. My passion is what I call skiting (Skates+Kites), which is big wheeled roller-skates with a kite at Frank Island on low tide, right in front of Chesterman Beach.

Tofino provides endless good times, and I love meeting people here because Tofino has some really beautiful people. I love the ambience, the amicability/friendships, the warm people that give you a chance to prove yourself, not too judging-which I love-at least you have a chance to present yourself and they decide whether they like you or not. It's a very open community, and I love it. And age doesn't matter here.

If I had ONE day in Tofino, I'd do skiting all day on Frank Island, then I'd enjoy a beer or two, enjoy the view, and finish with a nice fire.

I'm at the Co-op Gas Bar every week night, while I'm not skiting, come and say hi. Please support your local Legion, and shop here in Tofino, support local businesses instead of shopping in Port Alberni because that's the way we survive here is by having people shop locally and I do that every day.

~~~~~~

Hi, my name is **Jesse Blake**. I'm co-owner of **Wildside Grill**. My passions are my wife and daughters, surfing, and fly fishing.

I love Tofino because of its BIG sandy beaches and lots of surfable waves.

I am Wildside Grill's chef and restaurateur, and founding member of Long Beach Fly Fishers.

If I had ONE day in Tofino, I'd go surfing with my girls.

Come on down to **Wildside Grill** open from 9AM-9PM everyday.

~~~~~~

Hey, this is **Jess Taylor**, calling Tofino home since 2007, via the lower mainland and some other beautiful parts of BC.

I love it here because of the people who've made this paradise their home. I love waving at people driving by. I love smiling and saying "Good Morning" and "Hello" to people, like you do when you're on holiday. That's essentially what life feels like here. One long holiday.

If I had ONE day in Tofino, I'd go crabbing on the inlet, pretty much anything around the water, go on endless hikes… all favorite pastimes.

Luckily for me, I get to make a living by doing something I love as well, which is spending time with friends and making them feel better about themselves… aka, giving them good hair. Good hair makes anyone feel better.

I opened **Salty Dolls Hair Salon** the year I moved here. I was initially cutting hair on docks, in kitchens, in driveways, you name it! I've come to specialize in weddings, doing both hair and makeup. I book over a year in advance for brides, and have done work in film, TV, and print. Continually being there for the best day of people's lives is the most amazing job I could have. So aside from the best job ever, I teach surfing occasionally with **Surf Sister**, and play banjo in a band with some of my girlfriends. Our group is called Little Saturday.

Come by the shop and say hi if you're in town. You can pick up an album, a t-shirt, or maybe book in for some good hair.

107-605 Gibson St, Tofino
250-266-0266
www.Saltydollshairsalon.com

My name is **Jill Patterson,** and I do a little bit of everything in Tofino. I love to plan events, parties and weddings, take pictures, and make jewelry. I'm passionate about art, community, big trees, fresh air and the sea.

Tofino is an amazing place as it allows me to blend my work, leisure, and love. The lines are often blurred between having fun and making a living. Nature is literally out my front door. I love the constant sound of waves in the background, the support and inspiration from a community infused with creativity, and the endless activities and celebrations about town, throughout the year. We have an abundance of amazing eateries and a festival for pretty much EVERYTHING!

By day, I am an event coordinator at Jamie's Rainforest Inn. I plan parties, fundraisers, weddings, and more. For fun, I am a photographer and jewelry maker. The dark days of winter, you can find me swimming in beads or editing elopements. Tofino is one of the most beautiful places in the world. It's no wonder so many choose this locale to exchange their vows. See some of my work here: www.jillnancyphoto.com.

If I had ONE day in Tofino, I would start with a big breakfast at **Jamie's Restaurant & Lounge** while awaiting my bike delivery from **Bicycle Marc.** I'd pedal my way along the MUP (Multi Use Path) to town and check out some of the shops and galleries before grabbing my surf gear from **Long Beach Surf Shop.** Next stops would be the **Tofino Brewery** on industrial way for a growler, **Picnic Charcuterie** for a couple pepperoni sticks, then **Chocolate Tofino** for a thermos pint of salted caramel ice cream for later. I'd cruise down to North Chesterman Beach, grab a coffee from the Driftwood Lounge and pop by the carving shed to say hi to Feather George. I'd nestle amongst some driftwood with a blanket, beach fire, and my snacks, for a day of ocean dips and easy living.

～～～～～～～～～～～～～～～

Hello, I'm **Joe Martin.** My traditional name is Too tah qwees nup she tl, and I'm from the house of Ewos of Tla-o-qui-aht. The chief of Tla-o-qui-aht First Nation is my oldest brother; his name is Robert Martin. I come from this place, and I grew up in the village of Opisaht. My first boat ride ever was in a canoe when I was a tiny baby with my mom and dad.

Growing up in Opitsaht, I remember it was really awesome. I look back at when all of the elders would go into anyone's house. They were so respectful of the kids, "Does your mom know where you are? Are you hungry?" and they would go on like this, it was great! "Need something to drink?" It was beautiful when I was growing up. Everyone was so nice to all of the kids. The social and mental impact of the Residential School System started setting into many people coming out of those schools; so it began to deteriorate a lot. We've had to live with those conditions and heal from it. I think there's a similar phenomenon all across Canada. So the people here when I was growing up that's how it was. My father was one of the traditional chiefs of our tribe.

I love that my home is fairly healthy. We can still have clean water here. The air is beautiful and nice to breathe, and it's beautiful to wake up in the morning especially in the springtime with all the birds out. Even now, there are seabirds all around that still give me joy to see. I love seeing them, and nature here in this part of the world is beautiful. I've traveled to many other parts of the world and every time I come back here there is nothing like this place. This is my home.

I grew up with my father. When I was really young he didn't leave me a choice; he'd say, "Get ready! we are going fishing, seal hunting, or making canoes!" When I was young, I didn't want to go. I wanted to play on the beach with the boys. And Dad said, "Nope, get ready, we are going." He'd always be ready to give me a boot and say, "I told you to get ready." Because of him, I learned about the land, the oceans and all kinds of things. Then, as a kid, I didn't really like it, but now I really appreciate what I learnt and especially how to carve a canoe.

Starting at 18, I worked in logging camps for many years, until I was fired because I refused to drag some logs that had small salmon fry (eggs) in it across a stream. I was fired and became their worst enemy. I started to work with the WWF (World Wildlife Fund), the blockades. and developing Meares Island Tribal Park. I traveled to Europe several times to speak about the environmental impacts on native communities.

If I had ONE day in Tofino/Tla-o-qui-aht, I'd do what I do everyday. I'd wake up at 5AM., continue teaching about the land, our traditional teachings. Attend healing circles where people have been impacted by many different issues that arise here. It's important for people to do those things and to help them through it. It helps myself too, to become a better person.

I'd highly recommend going on a nature walk in Pacific Rim National Park with Gisele my daughter, or a dugout canoe tour offered by my youngest daughter Tsimka at *T'ashii Paddle School*. They've been in business 14-15 years or so, and I feel that those things are really important for people to get out to do, to learn about our culture, our history. There are other native tours for people to check out. There are people who have lived around these waters for thousands of years and know this land extremely well. And there are many people that operate boats daily on the water.

~~~~~~

Hi, we are **The Wynnes**, **John** and **Lise**. We own and operate **Castaways Value Store,** Tofino's community based re-selling, re-purposing, re-gifting store. Before purchasing Castaways in 2010 we operated a successful cleaning business for 15 years, serving many local businesses, institutions and households.

We met and fell in love with one another here in Tofino. We love the beauty, the freedom and most of all, the people of this place and their pets.

Lise manifests jewelry from semi-precious stones, crystals and kelp. She moved to Tofino 23 years ago, after spending 13 years' lighthouse keeping, where she cultivated creative endeavors, that became the art that she produces today. She uses watercolors, sculpts, and works with fabric and fibers. Currently she is making sage smudge wands in kelp and wanders to Lillooet to harvest the sage and jade. Her time on the lighthouses has taught her much about gardening, preserving and cooking.

Living in Tofino means being able to "be by yourself;" enjoying the fresh air after a torrential rainfall and the cheeriness of little brown birds, signaling that the sun is about to shine.

If we had ONE day in Tofino, we would go to the Hot Springs or Lise would love to simply lose herself in the sand dunes along Wickaninnish Beach.

www.castaways-tofino.com
email: castaways@telus.net
phone: 250-725-2004

Better still, come visit us at the store.
455 Campbell St. Tofino.
Our downtown garden courtyard awaits you.
Yours truly,
John and Lise

~~~~~~

Hi, my name is **Kate Crosby,** and I'm a mom of two kids and owner of Tofino Brand retail shop. I've been in Tofino for nine years. When I first arrived in Tofino, I was a little cranky because the drive was much longer than expected, but when I walked through the breezeway at Long Beach Lodge, I had tears in my eyes. That was it! The most perfect place in the whole world.

There is so much to love about Tofino. I love the feeling of space around me and that my children, since very young, are safe to play and roam around with limited restrictions. There is something about running on the beach that pulls out all sorts of emotions, and in a way, nature is in itself my therapist at times. This place works wonders. Then there is the water. To be out on the water is in itself amazing!

If I only had ONE day in Tofino, I would like to hike Lone Cone Mountain with my kids, Owen and Susi. We would have a picnic at the top and suck in the views for an hour or so before heading back down. We would then head over to Shelter Restaurant for dinner and wine (for me), and then I would go to the beach with friends and their families, watch the sunset, drink more wine, watch the kids run around, and enjoy it all till we're all conked out!

Please drop by my shop located at 455 Campbell Street, right next to Mermaid Tales Bookshop. Take home a wearable memory of this fantastic place. I'm open from 10 a.m.–4 p.m. and would love to hear how much you love this place too!

Kate Crosby
Tofino Brand Store
Business: 250-725-2256
Cell: 250-266-9020

My name is **Kate Sitka**, and I'm a spirit medium and animal communicator. Welcome to our wonderful town!

My partner Kathryn and I stumbled upon the wild West Coast while on vacation, and once we knew it existed we just couldn't live anywhere else! We hail from North Bay, Ontario, and we moved here in 2009 with two cats and two dogs.

I love Tofino & Ucluelet, the healthy life, the holistic values, and how everyone here takes care of each other.

If you had ONE day in Tofino, be sure to check out the Big Tree Trail on Meares Island, or the fabulous Hot Springs Cove, my very favorite place in the world!

I help people have conversations with their loved ones in spirit, and their pets who are alive or in spirit. People often want to talk to a friend or relative of theirs who has passed, and it's a real privilege to be a part of that conversation. Animal communication is often about bringing the human and the animal closer together, making sure everyone's needs are met. It's incredible what comes up during these sessions; it's like working in miracles! Most of my sessions are done over the phone, and so I especially love to do in-person readings with visitors.

If you're planning a visit and you'd like an in-person session, please book well in advance at tofinopsychic.com! The summer sessions fill up VERY quickly. If you can't find availability for your visit, you're welcome to email me tofinopsychic@gmail.com, and I may be able to sneak you in. You can find all of my information including tips for an effective reading, my blog, podcast, guest posts, coupons, seasonal specials, classes and all of my internet comings and goings on my website: **www.Tofinopsychic.com** Enjoy your stay!

My name is **Kati Martini** and I arrived in 1985, a time when the residents of Tofino and Opitsaht were telling the world about the ancient rainforests of Clayoquot Sound. For a kid from southern Ontario, the cedars of the coast were unforgettable. I returned to work as a naturalist in Pacific Rim National Park and was able to share my excitement about this special place with visitors from around the world. Now I get to do that as part of the crew at our tour company, Remote Passages Marine Excursions!

I love that in Tofino, I can call out 'slug alert' and mean it! Banana slugs are one of the 'charismatic megafauna' of the ancient rainforest in which Tofino is located. Stopping to let a slug cross is an opportunity to talk about its role in the rainforest complex, and the role of the rainforest in shaping the landscape, and the connection of the forest landscape to the ocean ... it's a naturalist/ interpreter thing.

My husband Don Travers and I own and operate **Remote Passages Marine Excursions** – Don runs the marine side of things, while I work land-side. Our company is about connecting people thoughtfully and respectfully with Tofino and Clayoquot Sound. We genuinely feel that connections to people all over the world will be part of the long-term protection for this special place. Getting guests out on the water by Zodiac to encounter a whale, or to observe a black bear and her cubs, or out by kayak to paddle the edges of the harbour islands at low tide and to walk the rainforest on Meares Island – these are the experiences we and our crew at 'Remote' love to create!

If I had ONE Tofino summer day, I would hop in a kayak on a low-tide morning to check out some colourful tide-pools just across the harbour. By mid-morning, it would be great to be out on the open coast by boat to see which gray whales are in the area – we know lots of them by name! And sea otters -- since I waited 15 years to see a sea otter in the wild on our coast, it's still a thrill for me every time we encounter them. Ready for lunch in town – so many great options in Tofino, and I can walk up to most of them in just a couple of minutes from our boathouse and dock on Wharf St. With a free afternoon, I might walk the rainforest trails at the **Tofino Botanical Gardens,** or head to Long Beach (my favourite area to explore is south from Comber's Beach), then grab a fish taco at **Wildside Grill** on my way back to watch the sunset from our dock. During storm season (November - February) I would spend my day with a copy of 'Chasing Clayoquot' (an amazing, inspiring almanac of the seasons in Tofino and the Sound, by David-Pitt Brooke; check **Mermaid Tales Bookshop** for this and many other great books by local authors) and a cup of coffee (**Common Loaf Bake Shop** or **Rhino Coffee House** to read and visit with neighbours, or a cappuccino from **Tofino Coffee** if taking a coffee to go).

Our tour company, **Remote Passages Marine Excursions,** launches daily March through the end of October from our boathouse and dock at 51 Wharf St. in Tofino. Guests love our extended "Hot Springs Explorer" whale and wildlife day excursion; families especially enjoy our half-day programs – whale watching or bear watching, or the 1.5 hour Meares Island 'Big Tree Trail' by Zodiac – and we can find an accessible guided sea kayak excursion for most guests. Call us at 1-800-666-9833 (or local 250-725-3330), or visit our website at **www.Remotepassages.com** for information and group rates.

My name is **Kayla McCloy**, local aspiring artist and happy barista at Tuff Beans Coffee House.

I love that Tofino is dog friendly everything! Hotels, patios, beaches! I love that we have an amazing sense of community. You never make it to your destination in the rain without being offered a ride. Eating out means eating local, fresh and not from a large franchise (McDs, etc.).

I'm a barista at **Tuff Beans.** In my spare time I volunteer anywhere I can! I would call myself the designated volunteer kids face painter for almost every event. I'm a foster home for rescues on their way to forever homes with the local care network. I teach the local kids art classes!

If I had ONE day in Tofino, I'd get on a boat and see Clayoquot Sound! Words cannot describe how beautiful it really is. The hot springs trips are a great way to see all the area has to offer.

~~~~~~

Hi, **Kevin Midgley** here, the glass guy of Tofino. I have been here over a decade and working with glass for over 35 years. My fused glass studio is special for those who love glass. I love chatting with visitors about what I make. Come and visit me and you may come away with a unique item for a special gift or remembrance of your visit to Tofino.

I love to walk the many beaches Tofino offers and eat at **SOBO**, the best restaurant in Tofino, just up the street from my studio. My favorite view is from the SOBO restaurant street corner looking out over the always changing ocean. It is a view I see every time I go the two blocks into town.

The four things a visitor has to do during a visit to Tofino are #1, 2, 3 Walk the beaches. #4 Visit Kevin's **Tofino Art Glass Studio** at 264 First Street located enroute to Tonquin Park. There you will find my handmade earrings, beach sand pendants, plates bowls and art pieces.

I'm open most days, most of the time, but open when open and closed when closed. Isn't that the way one should live life?

250-725-3929

~~~~~~

My name is **Krissy Montgomery** and I'm the owner and operator of **Surf Sister** and the co founder of the Queen of the Peak - Women's Surf Championships. My story is a common one. In 1998 I packed up my car and headed to the coast in search of surf and what I found was more than waves. I found a community of like minded people, a family of friends, and endless adventures...I found home and never left!

To me a perfect day in Tofino is still the same today as it was in 1998, only with better restaurants to choose from! A surf with friends, a hike with my dogs, and a good meal are hard to beat. My favorite weekend of the year has to be the first weekend in October when we host the Queen of the Peak. The contest highlights all the great female athletes and gives the surf community a chance to compete and celebrate. It's like setting a stage to watch my friends shine.

Surfing to me has always been more than just a sport. It has educated me about the environment, taken me on epic travels, and introduced me to community that I love. I hope while you are visiting Tofino, you swing by **Surf Sister** and let myself and my friends share our stoke with you!

My name is **Liam McNeil**, and I have the pleasure of paddling between old growth islands almost every day with Tofino Sea Kayaking. Tofino stole my heart over 15 years ago. I wandered across the mountain ranges of Vancouver Island and set down roots in the salty soil of the west coast.

Since 1988 **Tofino Sea Kayaking** has been the leader in sea kayaking in Clayoquot Sound, and with numerous local year-round guides we love showing visitors our home.

We specialize in day tours, multi-day tours, instructional courses, kayak rentals and more. Our store has incredible espresso, a view overlooking the harbour, art gallery and retail. As Tofino's original hotel a century ago, we still have accommodation upstairs in the Paddlers Inn.

If I had ONE day in Tofino, I would start with a hot espresso on our patio, head out on the water to sea kayak in Clayoquot Sound, and then head into town to enjoy an incredible meal, then go for an evening walk on the beach with my family. This is MY Tofino.

See you soon!

Tofino Sea Kayaking

320 Main St

250-725-4222

www.Tofinoseakayaking.com

info@tofinoseakayaking.com

Hi, my name is **Lilly Woodbury** and I am born and raised Tofitian. Life itself is an opportunity, for any species. It is a chance (albeit chances are not equal) to survive the elements, evolve, explore, cooperate and - if we are lucky - to thrive; meaning to grow vigorously. For Western society, especially since the industrial revolution, the interpretation of what it means to thrive has been grossly misunderstood. It has been twisted to become synonymous with extraction and domination of earth and all of its inhabitants in order to create monetary growth for very few people. A lot of us are familiar with how this narrative continues; it sounds a lot like a Grimm's fairy tale here in present-day Tofino. It sounds terrible yet distant and non-threatening in this beautiful town, a town where you can get lost amongst the waves and all the activities this landscape allows. However, we are not exempt from how the global economic system of capitalism has altered the planet, and this will only become more apparent with time, if we do not act wisely!

Considering the way of thriving, people live in Tofino to find a way to do just that. People fulfill their passions here, and often, undiscovered passions are ignited by living here. There is an uncanny amount of talented people for such a small area who have contributed to Clayoquot's symbol as an apex of aesthetic beauty. I believe this is a continuation of how the Nuu-chah-nulth Nations have been living here since time immemorial, being artistically inspired by the surroundings and being co-creators of the environment.

Unfortunately, the Nuu-chah-nulth way of living responsibly with the ecosystems from which we draw sustenance has been severed on a large scale; and there is a lot of work to do in order to regenerate healthy oceans, air, and soil. In Tofino, becoming part of the regeneration movement looks like changing the ways we deal with waste, growing more local food, becoming part of a post-carbon economy with the transition town movement, as well as getting involved in ecological restoration and monitoring projects, to name just a few. There is a plethora of ways we can immerse ourselves in this movement to change the system. (This is where you get up and chant: SYSTEM CHANGE, NOT CLIMATE CHANGE!)

This also applies for the travelers from near and far visiting Tofino. If people are going to use this precious present time to travel, it's essential to become involved in the regeneration of the place being visited. In Tofino, this could mean attending a workshop at **Tofino Botanical Gardens,** taking a course at **Raincoast Education Society,** going on a dugout canoe tour with **T'ashii paddle school,** attending a documentary at the local theatre, supporting the amazing **Mermaid Tales bookshop,** volunteering with one of the non-profit organizations like Clayoquot Action, One Kind Mind, and Friends of Clayoquot sound.

Whether living in Tofino or visiting, let's all use our talents and passions to thrive, to grow well by cultivating an ethic of respect and reciprocity with the earth.

~~~~~~

My name is **Lisa Ahier**, chef at **SOBO Restaurant**. I love to feed my community. I love teaching young people to cook.

I love the active lifestyle that Tofino affords. Great, great restaurants! I like that it's small enough to know everyone on a first name basis.

I am chef at SOBO. My brand is my cookbook and my frozen food line. My favorite charities are the Hospice Society and the Kids Lunch Program.

If I had ONE day in Tofino, I'd go stand up paddle boarding on the quiet side of Tofino. The mudflat area is underrated. It's very beautiful and serene.

Come down to SOBO Restaurant, open for lunch and dinner. **www.Sobo.ca**

~~~~~~~~~~~~~~~~~~~~~~~~~~~~~~~~~~

Hello! My name is **Lisa Fletcher** and I am a long time resident of Tofino. I am a jewellery artist here in town, as well as a local biologist with Central Westcoast Forest Society.

I love Tofino and the West Coast because of it's endless surrounding beauty, the ocean and of course, the community.

Making jewellery is my passion. I use sterling silver, gold and gemstones to create collections, as well as custom work such as engagement and wedding rings. I'm easily inspired by the natural environment around me.

If I only had ONE day in Tofino it would start at **Tofino Coffee Co,** followed by a flight to Hot Springs for a soak, and finished with a delicious dinner at **Kuma Restaurant.**

My work can be found at retail stores in Tofino; **Rubio, Caravan, Merge, Surf Sister** and the **Wickaninnish Inn**. For custom inquiries get in touch! www.Lisafletcher.ca

~~~~~~~~~~~~~~~~~~~~~~~~~~~~~~~~~~

My name is **Lutz Zilliken**, I've been living in Tofino for over 20 years. I own **The Fish Store & Oyster Bar** and West Pacific Seafoods. We provide seafood to the restaurants and the general public.

Since being here just over 20 years, I've watched Tofino slowly grow into a really cool community and there is just a little bit of everything in this town, that's what I love. It's right on the ocean, what more can you want?

If I had ONE day in Tofino, I'd get up at 5AM, head out on the boat by 6AM, go salmon fishing and halibut fishing, bring it all back in, cut it up process it, put it on the BBQ. Perfect day.

The Fish Store & Oyster Bar the best place with the freshest seafood in town. Open five days a week from 11:30AM 'til late. The store itself is open seven days a week.

～～～～～～～～～～～～～～～～

Hey, it's **Marcel Zobel** from the **Tree House Gift Company.** I first moved to Tofino in 1993 and have loved getting to know the vast and wonderful surroundings. I have travelled and lived in a lot of wonderful places around the world, and Tofino will always be at the top of my list.

I love Tofino because the list of places to explore, things to do, and friends to share adventures with just keeps growing out here. The end of the road is where the next adventure begins; whether you're visiting for the first time, or have returned many times, Tofino always provides a special memory. I really enjoy having or sharing something special that reminds me of a time or place, and the **Tree House Gift Company** has Tofino's best selection of unique West Coast inspired gifts, garments, jewellery, books, pottery, souvenirs, and more that will do just that.

If I had ONE day in Tofino, I would do my best to hit the beach, explore the forest, and spend some time on the water. I'd wind down with a stroll through the town, and stop in at the **Tree House Gift Company** to find that perfect something to take home or send to a friend that would remind me of Tofino.

We are centrally located at 305 Campbell Street beside the CIBC and across from the Co-op Grocery. Give us a call at (250) 725-4254, or visit our website at www.Treehousegiftstofino.com

~~~~~~

My name is **Marco Procopio**. I was born and raised in Italy where I lived until the age of 22. After learning how to surf, windsurf and kitesurf in my home town, I felt the need to move to the big Pacific Ocean and after exploring many places around the world, I fell in love with Tofino where I can pursue my passions.

I teach StandUpPaddleBoarding, outdoor and indoor fitness, and I cook. This is what I do for work, and if I don't walk the beach with my wife and my dog then I'm surfing beautiful waves or hiking a trail. After 10 years of being away from home, I can now say that Tofino is home.

Tofino has the most beautiful community in the world, kind and caring of each other and the environment, crafty and always happy. Tofino is the most peaceful place. You can always find a spot where you can be on your own immersed in nature. It's also heaven for water activities. Waves on one side, flat water around the peninsula and tidal waves in the inlet.

I teach outdoor fitness and paddle boarding for **Tofino Paddle Surf** because I believe that outdoor activities are the best to keep us healthy and happy at the same time. I also cook because I believe good food make us happy, brings everybody together and I love food. My specialties are pizza and Mexican food.

If I had ONE day in Tofino, I would go for coffee, then go for a walk on the beach. Stormy or sunny, it's always spectacular. Then I would go for a surf, and a hike. Then I would try some amazing food in one of the go-to businesses and then I would go stand up paddle boarding in the inlet. I would not miss sunset at the beach of course. I would top up my day with a beer at the brewery and dinner in one of the fantastic restaurants in Tofino.

~~~~~~~~~~~~~~~~~~~~~~~~~~~

Hey Tofino! This is **Marcy Young** the owner of **The Fish Store & Oyster Bar.** Originally from Port Alberni just across the pass. Twenty years ago I came this way and now I work and live the Tofino Dream.

I love that Tofino has an amazing community where everyone is a neighbour, as well as a friend. The food scene is insane, which I am proud to be a part of and provide to locals and tourists. We are so lucky to be in such proximity to the outdoors in this beautiful area.

I own a small fish store and restaurant as well as a seafood processing plant. We are blessed to have amazing seafood in Tofino and we strive to provide the best product to our guests. Whether they join us in the restaurant for some grub or have their sport fishing catch processed to take home.

If I had ONE day in Tofino, that's an easy one; I'd have morning coffee on the beach with my dog Oscar and my man Lutz then offshore fishing for the day. There is nothing wrong with heading to the river for some steelhead action.

The Fish Store & Oyster Bar is located at 368 Main St. Come and join us for something to eat or the take home. You can contact the restaurant at 250-725-2264 or the plant at 250-725-2244.

Hi, I'm **Mark Hobson.** I've lived and painted in Tofino, B.C. for over 30 years. I was drawn to this outer coast community by the dramatic beauty and variety of the landscape, which is strongly reflected in my work. Originally a biologist and high school teacher, I taught myself skills in watercolour, oil and acrylic, becoming a full time artist in 1987. I'm best known for my use of light in my portrayals of Canada's remote West Coast and especially for my accurate underwater scenes inspired by scuba diving.

I love Tofino for: The people and community. The dramatic beauty and variety of the landscape. The remoteness.

If he had ONE day in Tofino, I'd take a boat trip through the inlets and islands to find some spots to set up and paint outdoors.

Mark Hobson Gallery
366 Campbell St.
Toll Free 1-800-668-2208
www.Markhobson.com

~~~~~~

Hi my name is **Markus Pukonen,** and I'm currently circumnavigating the earth without a motor raising support for local non-profits at www.routesofchange.org. I came to Tofino six years ago to be with my nieces, surf, and plan this 80,000 km(49,709.70 mi) five-year journey.

Living in Tofino sometimes feels like a dream, filled with eccentric characters, oversized trees, talkative whales, and an abundance of empty waves. I love that I can walk or ride my bike everywhere that I need to go, especially to the surf.

If I only had ONE day in Tofino, I would spend most of the day on the beach figuring out how I can stay longer. Then I would go for a canoe with **T'ashii Paddle School,** get some lunch at Green Soul, go for a surf, and finish the day with a **Wolf in the Fog** dinner.

If you're interested in joining me for an adventure as I bike, pogo stick, ski, hand cycle, dance, etc., please find me @routesofchange on Instagram/Snapchat/Twitter/Facebook/. I believe we can create a sustainable way of life on earth, and have fun while we do it!

Help me reach my goal to raise $10 million for a healthy future and contact me or donate at www.routesofchange.org

Enjoy Tofino!

~~~~~~

Hi my name is **Max Plaxton,** a former Olympian, born and raised in beautiful Tofino-BC. At age 11, I moved to Chile with my family, followed by Spain, but we would always come back to Tofino every year for the summer. I'm grateful I have been able to see much of the world, but it made me appreciate more then anything how stunning and amazing Tofino really is.

I love Tofino for the sense of community, the accessibility to the ocean/surf, and the amazing seafood. My mom used to call me and friends growing up "free range chickens" referring to the way we could just be out and about in such a safe place surrounded by such caring Tofitians. I was fortunate to get into surfing at a young age, something that has stuck with me to this day and will forever remain my passion! Growing up in Tofino, it was hard not to be surrounded by some of the best seafood in the world. Much of my family are involved in the industry, and it's a really huge part of the community, plus it's so good for you.

I was a professional athlete for 15 years! It was an amazing experience, but like all good things it had to come to an end. I'm now involved in the commercial fishing industry specifically geoduck harvesting. It's a delicacy of a shellfish and I recommend everyone to try it!

If I had ONE day in Tofino, I would sleep in a little because I don't sleep anywhere in the world but Tofino! I'd then ride my bike (weather dependent of course) to **Tofino Coffee** and grab a cappuccino. I'd then check the surf with my dog and hopefully score some good waves and I'd follow that up with some **Tacofino** and perhaps a little siesta :) I'd try to save a little energy for another sunset surf or a walk on the beach and then grab some eats at **Shelter** with some good company and of course cold **Tofino Brewing** beers.

~~~~~~

Hi my name is **Michelle Hall** and I live in Tofino with my husband Alan, and together we run a wellness and recreation retreat called **Cedarwood Cove.** We moved here in 2013 after many years of driving to the end of the road, to surf the wild west coast and to be immersed in nature, escaping the concrete. Alan proposed to me on Chestermans Beach in 2013, and we were moved and married in the same spot three months later. It was love!

We open our home to guests around the world and invite them to relax, play and rejuvenate in the serene surroundings we are so lucky to live in. Our home is on the Tofino inlet waters, and you can lose hours watching the never-ending stream of birds, eagles, wolves, bears, seals and nature pass by. We offer yoga, massage, stand up paddling, nutritional services, rentals for bikes and surf gear as well as hosting retreats throughout the year.

Waking up to the sunrise over the mountains and practicing yoga on the deck with the song of the birds, drinking tea in silence at the end of the jetty watching the tide come in, taking a paddle board out and having an adventure around the islands, cooking fish on the fire pit with new friends, watching the stars appear in the darkness, feeling part of everything...This is MY TOFINO.

Come and watch stars with us? www.cedarwoodcove.ca

Michelle Hall
Wellness Host @ Cedarwood Cove
Registered Holistic Nutritionist (RHN)
Licensed Bodyworker, RYT 200 Yoga Alliance

~~~~~~

My name is **Monte Clarke,** and I work at **Storm Surf Shop**. My role is to be with the people! I guess you can say I am store manager.

I love Tofino for its community, rawness of the nature, and the overall beauty of the whole place.

I surf, I work at Storm, I am here for the people, the community, the locals to get their surf gear.

If I had ONE day in Tofino I would be in the ocean! And if I had time, I would go to all of the local businesses to say hi; get coffee at different shops, go in the surf shops, check out the restaurants, whale watching, and hot springs.

Come see me down at Storm Surf Shop, we are open from 10-5PM in the summer time, 10am-5PM in the winter. You can reach us online www.stormcanada.ca , via email or phone us at (250) 725-3344.

~~~~~~

Greetings! I am a wild woman roaming the west coast of Vancouver Island. My parents named me **Morgan**, middle name Leigh (which means "from the sea") and I was given my father's last name, which is Callison. Some people call me The Morning Light, other people call me Morgan. When interpreted, my name means Morning From The Sea...which is quite fitting as I came from the East Coast all the way across Canada to find my second home on the wild West Coast...from the sea to the sea.

I came to Tofino on a whim, many years ago...and quickly decided this was the town that I had always been looking for, even though I was never looking. I found what my heart needed and what my soul was calling for.

This town has allowed me to awaken to my passions by supporting all of the crazy, fun and sometime practical ideas that I've come up with. Opening an organic food store has fuelled my passion for health and nutrition while offering me a space to truly connect with this community. Green Soul Organics is one of my passions and it has given me the resources to connect with many of my other passions...visual art, dancing, writing, cooking, hosting community events, and living life in a very full and deep way.

And why stop with the store...why not take it a step farther and co-create an organic take out cafe with a bunch of awesome women... **Earth Mama Love Kitchen Collective** was born out of a dream to work cooperatively with other like-minded and like-hearted individuals, all coming together to support a healthy community that is based on equality, self empowerment on all levels and sweet loving intentions. These are all flourishing personal passions!

And now that these are in full swing...I realized I can semi-retire at 33 and explore more deeply my passion for creative soul writing and creative soul painting...these two forms of creative expression bring me immense joy...you can find out more on FB under Morgan Leigh Callison or come into my shop Green Soul Organics and find some of my works available there.

I love the vibrancy that shines forth from the people of this town. The glow, the shimmer and the shine that we all possess as we stretch ourselves to awaken our dreams into reality. I love the authentic laid back nature that says, "life is for living, for learning and for loving...slow down, be present, enjoy this time that is your life." I love the fact that Tofino is built on first nations land ... because it means that I have been exposed to their traditional ways of life, through healing ceremonies, through the sharing of arts and culture and through hearing the stories that they tell. There is so much ancient knowledge here, and that has been a huge inspiration for me to find my own inner wisdom. I am truly grateful to be here on this land, doing what I am doing while living alongside such beautiful people.

Every day to me is ONE Day in Tofino...so everyday I try to do what I really want to do. What I really feel like doing. Sometimes it's as simple as spending the day in my cabin alone, reflecting, healing and creating. Sometime I feel the pull to the ocean or deep into the forest and then I go. Sometimes I want to spend the day working and then have dinner with friends ... but in the end, if I had just one day, I'd do whatever it was I felt like doing right then ... my aim with every day is to be present, do what I love and love those around me.

If I had one wish for this community as it becomes more and more driven by tourism, is that the tourist/community engagement strengthens with each passing season...I want to make eye contact with the people I pass on the street, even if I don't know them. I want to see tourists at community events, not as spectators, but as participants...I wish to see the bridge be built that brings us all together, strengthening all of our connections to the land, the people and this life. I wish for the tourists to see all the aspects of this community that make this place so very special.

Love, Peace & Joy, Morgan Leigh Callison

~~~~~~

I'm **Nate Laverty.** I am a filmmaker, based in Tofino, BC. I am passionate about all things creative, the outdoors, sunny mornings, coffee and surfing.

I love Tofino because everyone is so friendly. There are a lot of nice places with nice people, but Tofino people are more than just nice. They're friendly. Its proximity to Vancouver is also nice because it allows me to live in the best place on earth, but get to work real quick thanks to **Orca Airways.**

I create and shoot short films, action sports pieces and commercial spots. I do it because it's my form of expression. Everything I imagine, feel, see and hear becomes a piece of what I create.

If I had ONE day in Tofino, I would surf, drink Tofino coffee, go to Lisa Fletcher's studio, say hi to Monte and the gang at Storm, hike Cox Lookout and sleep in a tree.

I am Nate Laverty, filmmaker at **Realtimeproductions.co.** Tofino completes all of my creative processes and gives me the outdoor experiences that refresh and rejuvenate my soul.

Hi, my name is **Nicole Botting**. I'm born and raised in Tofino along with my four brothers and parents for the last 21 years. Growing up in a small town has taught me the importance of family and community, and my years living here have taught me the kindness a small town can teach you.

I love the opportunities I have every year to meet new people, and yet at the same time always still be able to enjoy the parts of Tofino that I loved growing up as a child. Growing up in this community has allowed me to become a part of so many families here, and through that I have discovered a love for childcare, which is a growing passion of mine.

If I had ONE day in Tofino, my ideal day would be spending the day enjoying all the best that Tofino has to offer, such as the locally owned restaurants, being with my family out on the beaches, enjoying the secret local hikes that are almost untouched. Mostly just experiencing all the beautiful things that have brought my family and friends to live here, and be together in one of the most amazing places this country has to offer.

Hey! I'm **Nicole Lohse**. I left the mountains and moved to Tofino in 2013 and knew as soon as I got here that it was where I belonged. When the ocean calls, you've got to follow! As a surfer, yoga instructor and Feldenkrais Practitioner I love that my 'jobs' consist of inspiring others to play, be curious and explore what they're capable of.

Tofino to me is Canada's Hawaii. Here we are reminded that we are just small beings amongst something so vast and beautiful. I feel we are all drawn here for similar reasons – reasons that are felt more then they can be explained. A feeling of being connected to nature, to a community, to something greater. You'll have to come here to truly understand!

If I had ONE day in Tofino, I would start my morning off with a surf to enjoy the sunrise from the water. Breakfast would be a couple chocolate croissants and a hot chocolate from Tofino Coffee. Then it would be time for an adventure! I'd pack a picnic full of cheeses and meats from Picnics Charcuterie and head to Schooner Cove to sit in the sun and take in the views. On my way home I'd hop back in the water for another cheeky surf. Next stop would be the Brewery to have a casual beer with some friends. I'd take another beer to go and head out to Tonquin to watch the sun set. Then it'd be off to dinner at **Wolf in the Fog**!

I'd love to share my knowledge and passions with you. If you are looking for custom private yoga or Feldenkrais classes or wanting to improve your surfing, get in touch!

You can learn more on what it is I love to do at **fittorip.com** or **www.playingintheelements.com** or track me down at Surf Sister!

~~~~~~

My name is **Ocean Simone Shine**. I am a mother and have lived in Tofino for over 22 years. I first visited here when I was seven years old. It captured my heart and imagination from a young age. I crave being outside, following wolf tracks on rainy days, camping, fishing from my kayak and photographing people in love.

I love Tofino because this area is raw and wild. It's a playground where forest and ocean collide. Its power and beauty are humbling. This place touches people in extraordinary ways.

I am general manager of an adventure tour company - Ocean Outfitters. I am a photographer for **Douglas Ludwig Photography,** and I run an earthy vacation rental - Tonquin Beach Suite.

If I had ONE day in Tofino, I would get out on the water and explore the coastline! I'd look for whales or bears, and I'd graze some of the amazing food around town. I would end my day watching the sunset from Pettinger Point or Spirit Rock at the south end of Cox Bay.

If you want a quiet get away in the best part of town, please stay with me at the Tonquin Beach Suite. If you're getting married in Tofino and want your special day captured in a soulful story telling fashion, we are instinct driven photographers in creative pursuit of unusual compositions, light and human emotion. www.douglasludwigphotography.com

~~~~~~

Hi, my name is **Pascale Froment**. I love the ocean, going on adventures, spending time in nature, yoga and delicious food! Luckily Tofino is the perfect place to explore all these passions. Born and raised here on the beach in the early '80s and now I'm looking forward to raising a family with my loving, adventure-seeking partner Ryan!

If I had ONE day in Tofino, I would get out in or on the ocean, enjoy some of the amazing food and then head to a yoga class! Oh and a hike, trip to the hot springs, beach walk, sushi, education on the natural environment, there are so many wonderful options!

At **Live to Surf,** our family owned and operated surf shop since 1984, we offer surf lessons, rentals, sales, and group rates. Stop by for a surf report, say hello and browse our selection of surf, skate, stand up paddle and body boards.

Catch a yoga class with us at **Coastal Bliss Yoga**, established in 2010 with daily drop in classes, special events and a cozy space to rent for your own yoga offerings. Also available group and private classes as well as beach and SUP yoga in the summer months. Both are conveniently located in the same area, Outside Break, with yummy food establishments you must check out - **Chocolate Tofino, Wildside, Tofitian Coffee Shop, Tacofino** and other shops.

Welcome to TOFINO! Let the lines between you and nature get blurry while being respectful of the environment. Enjoy!

Live to Surf
250-725-4464
livetosurf.com
info@livetosurf.com

Coastal Bliss Yoga
1-888-589-2246
coastalblissyoga.com
info@coastalbissyoga.com

both located at 1180 Pacific Rim Hwy

My name is **Phil Reimers**. I've lived in Tofino for four years at the **Tofino Botanical Gardens.** My passions are building and crafting with wood, alternative energy, the movement art of Aikido and dancing.

I love Tofino for the very beautiful forests and landscapes. Tofino has a young and inspiring community, with lots of great people and projects.

I work in the Garden, managing the lodge and constructing/ landscaping. It is a good combination of office work and hands on. I like the spirit of the Tofino Botanical Gardens, and I'm happy to be a part of it.

If I had only ONE day in Tofino, I'd go see the sunrise on the mudflat, then have coffee at **Darwin's Café.** Surf and after that a sauna. Breakfast at **Long Beach Lodge,** lunch at **Tacofino** and dinner at **Wolf in the Fog** or **Shelter**. At the end of the day, go see the sunset at Chestermans and start a beach fire.

~~~~~~~~~~~~~~~~~~~~

My name is Rhonda, aka **Rhonda Lily**. I've been a local Tofitian since 2005 and have no plans to leave anytime soon, why would I?!

I have travelled to many places and this is by far my favorite. Mystical rainforest, ocean as far as the eye can see, endless sandy beaches, snow capped mountains, wildlife, wild people, indigenous culture and wisdom and some of the best restaurants, coffee, and chocolate in the Pacific North West.

I love yoga and nature. I am ever grateful for the community, my craft (hairstylist) and my business, **Studio One Tofino (Aveda Concept Salon)** for supporting my beautiful life style here in Tofino.

I encourage everyone to come and experience the bliss and magic that is found here; your heart and soul will thank you. Me and my team at Studio One would love to enhance your experience with many beautifying services!

www.studioonetofino.ca
250-725-3450
Located between Live to Surf and Wildside Grill.

~~~~~~~~~~~~~~~~~~~~

Hi! My name is **Ryan Stewart**. I came to Tofino three years ago and instantly fell in love with life here! The island has been my home my whole life, and Tofino is the icing on the cake!

Despite how busy Tofino can be, I love it for the quiet moments, listening to the ocean crashing on shore, fishing up the inlets with friends, and going for daily beach walks with my dog Ginger.

I am a deckhand for Wichita Towing, and prior to that for Aquatic Safaris. I love being on the water, in the outdoors, seeing the sunrise behind Meares Island, and set on the open ocean, I feel at home there.

If I had ONE day in Tofino, I would take a boat out to Cannery Bay and then cruise up to Sydney Inlet and visit Hot Springs Cove, and when we returned I would finish with sushi at **Tough City Sushi!**

~~~~~~

My name is **Samantha Hackett**, director of operations at **Long Beach Lodge Resort**. I moved to Tofino January 2008 and met my now husband that first week! It was my first move out of my home town of Victoria, and I immediately fell in love. I fell in love with the supportive community, the lush lively environment, the Lodge's family style work culture, and of course the love of my life.

If I had only ONE day in Tofino I would get outside and enjoy the beach, beautiful rain or shine. I would slurp up some freshly shucked local Clayoquot Climax oysters with a glass of British Columbia wine. And a trip out on the water with a whale sighting would be icing on the cake!

Tofino is a special place and I enjoy sharing it with visitors from all over the world.

Come visit us at the Lodge and enjoy one of our cozy luxurious rooms, inspired cuisine with inspiring Pacific vistas, exclusive "catch of the day" marine tours, or discover the joy of surfing. Long Beach Lodge Resort offers two year-round styles of accommodation, two bedroom cottages or a room in our beachfront lodge. Arguably one of the best "rooms" on North America's Pacific coastline, our Great Room offers a place to escape, put your feet up and relax and has food and drinks available for breakfast, lunch, après surf, and dinner. And in the summer the SandBar Bistro is Tofino's ultimate outdoor, beachside patio, offering casual table or to-go food service and licensed beverage service with incredible sunsets! Long Beach Lodge Resort is Tofino's luxury adventure resort offering an on-site surf club (lessons, & rentals) and customized marine wildlife boat tours.

Samantha Hackett, Director of Operations
Long Beach Lodge Resort
PO Box 897, 1441 Pacific Rim Hwy
Tofino BC V0R 2Z0
(250) 725-2442
www.longbeachlodgeresort.com

My name is **Shandy Kariatsumari**. I have a seven-year-old daughter, various jobs I am passionate about, and have lived in Tofino 20 years. I home school my daughter with a Waldorf curriculum, run out to the surf any chance I get, and compete in surf events.

I was born and raised in a small riverside town called Rocky Mountain House in the Alberta Prairies. I grew up focusing on competitive swimming with the tiniest exposure to the West Coast. It was when I was in Nationals with University of Calgary that I began to explore further. After acceptance to Emily Carr

University of Art and Design in Vancouver, I retired from swimming and discovered surfing. In my final year I created a course to apprentice with surfboard shaper Billy Leech. This graduation project allowed me to live in Tofino, commute to ECIAD school, and eventually travel the North American Western Coastline and to international countries for surfing. Keeping Tofino as home-base, I pursued many new interests, growing with the inspiration of a young community.

Surfing was, and still is, a big reason why I love living in Tofino. It is challenging to surf well here, yet there is always a wave, a natural landscape, and unlimited potential. Tofino opens my eyes to First Nations folklore; it deepens a conversation with my environment. My daughter and I love the rainforest moisture, mild climate, and young family community all supportive in fun adventures or nature based lifestyle. We feel warmed by Tofino. We interact with small devoted businesses and live appreciatively witnessing the growing multitude of talents each person in this community continues to show up with.

I work as an individual affiliate offering Lifesaving Bronze Medallion and Cross Courses. We practice mainly in the ocean with pool time for ages 13 and up. Mostly, I create an upgraded version for adult surfers to meet the requirements for surf instruction at any one of the many surf schools in Tofino.

I manage **Live to Surf School**, training our surf instructors, and overseeing a variety of duties. I work at Small Miracles, a home based, natural daycare.

I work at Tofino Nature Kids, an outdoor program at **Botanical Gardens** and North Chesterman Beach. Its design is inspired by Jon Young's 8 Shields Coyote Mentoring. In link with Tofino Nature Kids, we run a Parent and Tot program in my home 'school room', giving connection to Nature and Waldorf Pedagogy.

I surf as a team rider for Live to Surf.

All of these businesses and roles are a means to live inspired and empower others likewise. I want others to feel what it means to be prepared, to sense an opening in their heart, while they skillfully experience something new with courage.

If I had ONE day in Tofino, I'd get outside and soak up the quiet spaces, explore to experience without knowing the end result, forage and fine dine.

Hi there! My name is **Shawna Roberts**. I've lived in Tofino on and off for 20 years. No matter where I travel in the world, Tofino always calls me back. This is my home.

I love Tofino for how small I feel here. Living at the end of the road, surrounded by wilderness, I am constantly reminded of the power of nature. Encountering a black bear in the forest, swimming in phosphorescence or standing next to a tree hundreds of years old, it is impossible to forget that humans are intrinsically connected to the rest of the natural world.

In 2014, my husband Jay and I founded **Tofino Nature Kids** – a nature connection program for local and visiting children. Our goal is simple – to foster respect for the natural world by sharing the magic of this place that we call home. We can often be found looking for crabs on the mudflats, hugging big trees or playing in the waves with our two young daughters and the children in our programs. Come join us for an unforgettable experience of Tofino – warning, you might get muddy!!

Contact us at: info@tofinonaturekids.com, 250-725-2544, **www.tofinonaturekids.com**

~~~~~~

Hi my name is **Sheila Orchiston**, wife, mother, and owner of **Rare Earth Weddings** and **The Wedding Place**. My husband and I had been visiting Tofino for over 15 years when we finally decided it was time to move here. Initially we moved for the beauty of the place, the ocean, the rainforest, and now we can't leave because of the beauty of the people that live here!

I love Tofino for the people…so many stories, so many lives, so many travels. Tofino attracts amazing people and there is such a sense of community. Friends become family!

I love the natural beauty and the preciousness of it that is so apparent here in Tofino. Being so close with nature reminds me to 'take it all in and breathe it in' every day. It truly makes you remember what is important.

I love the food! It is crazy how we have so many incredible chefs in this small town. Having travelled many parts of the world, we are spoiled by the culinary experience here in Tofino. So much thought put into the food and ensuring it is local and organic. I appreciate it every day.

Every day I have the pleasure of working with couples from all over the world who choose Tofino for their wedding destination. I own and operate Rare Earth Weddings and The Wedding Place. I love helping people plan their wedding celebrations and showcase Tofino to them and their guests. My goal is to make planning their special day easy so that they can enjoy the moments along the way.

If I only had ONE day in Tofino, I would wake up early, kiss my husband and son, grab a coffee from **Tofino Coffee Company** or my friends at **Rhino Coffee House** and then head to the beach for a long walk. After that I would get in a kayak and kayak around Meares Island and hike Big Tree Trail. (Nothing is better than being on the water with a stop in the forest.) After lunch I would indulge in a massage at **Sacred Stone Spa** and then back onto the water with my friend Lochie at Tofino Fish Guides or Blake with Cleanline Sportsfishing and grab some prawns/crab and fresh fish for dinner with friends. Stop by the brewery for a growler of blonde lager and then have a campfire on Chesterman Beach with all those I love. Enjoying the sunset, the view of the islands and the epic starscape above on a clear night ... the sky is unreal with no lights from the city, just sitting and chilling with nature and my crew.

For wedding, elopement or honeymoons we offer customized packages based on your vision and budget. At our storefront "The Wedding Place" we have décor rentals, local artisan gifts, wedding party gifts, etc. Everything you need for a wedding or celebration. We can connect you with vendors and venues or book you into activities. We focus on local sustainable products from incredibly talented Tofitians. Come and check us out at our shop – **Rare Earth Weddings and The Wedding Place,** Unit 7- 368 Main Street or give us a call at 250-522-0087. For planning services, we offer a complimentary initial meeting!

My name is **Sophie Laboissonniere**. I moved to Tofino in 2014 to explore British Columbia's rich coast line. By doing so, I have enriched my connection with nature, community and understanding of British Columbia's abundant natural resources.

My ultimate favorite aspect of Tofino is experiencing all four, very unique seasons of the year. Each season gives me an understanding of the transient behavior of nature at its finest degree.

My experience in Tofino has provided me with a deeper understanding, and connection to my body. Because Tofino is entrenched with clean, green resources, it has empowered me to take initiative to follow specific health care regimes.

If I had ONE day in Tofino, I would walk the beaches and gaze as far back to the ocean as I could see. This action alone provides mystical wonder and amazement of the world we live in.

Living in Tofino has made me more aware of my surroundings, has giving me a deeper connection to my body and has encompassed what a true, loving community feels like. To those who are travelling to Tofino, or those who are thinking of moving to this luscious part of the globe, remember to respect this land, to respect the Tla-o-qui-aht First Nations and respect those who have been born and bred in this magical place.

~~~~~~

Hi! My name is **Sophie L'Homme,** and I've been back in Tofino since July 2015. I was in Montreal for the last six years, but the ocean was calling me back. I live in a tiny cabin on Chesterman Beach. I was pretty lucky to score a house so close to beach. I love going for walks on the beach to find sea treasures.

I'm so happy to be living in Tofino again. It's the perfect place for nature lovers who want be part of an awesome community and still want to have a social life! People say Tofino is a really rainy town but it's not "that" true. Winter still bring us some glorious sunny days that are perfect for lovely beach walks. It's awesome to be living in this remote town but still be able to go out for amazing food and drinks at night. I'm really proud of all the creative souls we have around here! People want to make a difference in this small town, and continually cultivate it into the awesome place that it is!

I'm so happy that I get to share my passion for music with Tofitians. I'm a professional jazz singer and composer. I have people coming to my tiny cabin for private singing lessons, piano lessons or music theory lessons. I also started the Tofino Children's Choir and Tofino Adult Choir. It's pretty awesome to have the kids and then the adults come singing around the grand piano of the theater with me every week. I also find the time to work a few other jobs. I drive a water taxi for Ocean Outfitters. I bring people to Meares island to either hike Lone Cone or the Big Tree Trail. I also work at Caravan Beach Shop (the cutest little store in town).

If I only had ONE day in Tofino, I would definitely go for a beach walk at low tide on Chesterman, go for a surf at Cox Bay and take a boat trip with Ocean Outfitters, the best whale watching company in town, to see the wildlife, and scenery! Great boats and great drivers/guides. I would end my day at Kuma for a yummy Japanese dish and then go to Wolf in the Fog for a Cedar Sour. Best drink in town!

If you are interested in singing, piano or theory lessons, please write me an email at sophielhomme@gmail.com. You can book a trip to Meares Island calling Ocean Outfitters at (250) 725-2866. They are located at 368 Main Street. You can come see me at Caravan beach shop. We are open Thursdays through Mondays from 10:30 to 5:30. Caravan is located at 346 Campbell Street.

My name is **Steve Dennis II**. My role/ passion is to have fun and enjoy life.

I love Tofino because it is my home. I love the culture of the surrounding communities. Tofino is family to me.

I do boating as much as my pocket can afford.

If I had ONE day in Tofino, I'd surf and go fishing.

Just come on down to the Whisky Dock (First Street) and look for the friendliest red skin and it's most likely me.

~~~~~~

Hey there, my name is **Tamo Campos,** and like the orcas that pass the shores, I'm a Tofino transient. I'm the co-founder of **Beyond Boarding,** a collective of snowboarders and surfers standing up for environmental and social justice across the province. We make documentary films, write articles in outdoor magazines and organize with frontline communities.

I love the pace of life in Tofino. From the laid back vibes of the community to the pounding waves of winter swell, there is always reason to come back.

I've also been incredibly inspired by the Tla-o-qui-aht and their tribal park initiative. In a world where we are facing environmental degradation, cultural assimilation and climate change, indigenous knowledge and territorial responsibilities can lead us on a humble path towards justice and sustainability. The Tla-o-qui-aht Tribal Parks inspires me because it is being lead, guided and put forth by the Tla-o-qui-aht people. I look forward to seeing it grow in the upcoming years.

I dedicate most of my life to environmental justice because it gives my life purpose. There are heavy times no doubt, but the waves and beauty of Tofino gives me the energy to keep going. We're so fortunate to live where we live. The wild salmon migrations, the animals, the fresh air and clean water are not ours to exploit but rather was passed down to us because of the stewardship of those that came before us. It's our turn to play our part. The growing movement against oil and gas tankers on our coast is our generation's fight to win.

If I had ONE day in Tofino, I'd surf at Long Beach, eat local seafood and chocolate and catch the sunset with a beach fire .

If you're interested in learning more about our work with Beyond Boarding visit our website www.beyondboarding.org or check us out on Facebook. Happy surf days!!

~~~~~~

Hi, my name is **Tanya Berger**. I moved to Tofino five years ago for surfing. I now am raising my two-year-old daughter and crafting beeswax candles. My business is called **Cloud Factory.**

One of the many reasons why I love Tofino is the people in our community; most of the locals are creative entrepreneurs who are happy to live here and aren't afraid to support each other's passions. I think the lack of distraction allows people to think and push their inspirations to do what is right for them.

The strong connection to the ocean and old growth rain forest is also one of the main reason why I love this place; it simply makes you feel alive.

If I had only one day to spend in Tofino, I would get up early, grab a coffee, stop by the Surf Sister shack at **Pacific Sands Resort** for a surf check, go for a surf, ride my bike to town with my daughter, have lunch at **Rhino**, stop by and say hi to my friends at **Storm**, grab my dog and head out to Schooner Cove for a hike, go for dinner at **Wolf in the Fog** and finish off with a sunset beach walk on Mackenzie beach.

I wanted to create a sustainable product and make people feel good about buying my product. Candle making is my craft and part of my lifestyle. I love going to the bee farms. I harvest my packaging elements on my hikes with my dog and daughter. I go say hi to staff and friends when I pick up beer bottles from the local resorts, I come home cut the bottles and craft my product.

We are lucky to live in this beautiful place and with everything that is happening in this day and age, I truly believe in GIVING BACK. For each candle sold, $1 is donated to a charity to protect our rainforest, to give back.

The Cloud Factory candles are made with 100% Vancouver Island beeswax, pure essential oils and some sand from one of our beautiful beaches, allowing you to bring a small part of Tofino into your home. Every candle is packaged in a recycled beer bottle and carefully covered with harvested fallen rainforest elements to preserve the candle.

For product or contact information, please visit my website, www.cloudfactorytofino.com.

~~~~~~

Hi! My name is **Tanya Dowdall,** and I came from the very east coast (NFLD & NS) to the very west coast as a National Park Warden in 2001. I am extremely grateful to live in Tofino and work in Pacific Rim National Park Reserve where my job is to do what I love: protect nature, cultural resources, and your experiences of this very special and unique place.

I love Tofino because it combines the best qualities of a small town (warmth, friendliness, and supportiveness) with the best features of a city (great restaurants, services, and entertainment) and is surrounded by wild, raw nature. Tofino is a place where the edges of many worlds meet, and that meeting creates an energy that attracts all kinds of life and a great diversity of people from around the world. Once here, you don't have to go far to experience any one of those worlds, and therein lies its beautiful simplicity. It's a powerful place.

If I had only ONE day to experience this place, I would watch the sunrise over Cox Bay from Middle Chesterman's. I would then walk up the beach to the **Driftwood Cafe** at the Wick Inn and get a mocha and pastry which I would either enjoy by the fire inside or on the beach out front as the sun warmed it. Next, I would get out on the water for the remainder of the morning and early afternoon, whether it was to go whale-watching, fishing, to the hot springs, to explore a remote beach or trail, or to go kayaking or surfing. Upon returning to town, I would go to **Chocolate Tofino** and get a chocolate elixir if it were winter, and chocolates or ice cream if it were summer, and then I would pack a picnic and hike down the Schooner Cove Trail to experience some rainforest and big trees. At the bottom of the trail, I would continue on out to Schooner Cove to enjoy some relatively unpeopled beach and ocean time to eat my picnic, swim, surf, sunbathe, read, nap, look, listen, relax, meet wildlife, whatever the season dictated. In summer, the days are long enough to do both of these morning and afternoon adventures but in winter, you would have to choose. At the end of the day, I would go out for dinner - Tofino has many great options to choose from. If I were feeling tired after dinner and at the end of this full day, I would return to my accommodation and soak in a hot tub under the stars or pouring rain, both are beautiful!

~~~~~~

Welcome to Tofino! We are the **team at Pacific Surf Co.,** a locally owned and operated surf shop that was founded in 1998. Our tight-knit, fun-loving and experienced PSCo. family all come together in Tofino for the same reasons – we love this town's sense of community; we love the natural environment, and we love the surf.

PSCo. places significant importance on company employee satisfaction and community involvement. Our team feels more like a family, and our lessons more like a fun day out in the water with friends. A perfect day for many of us includes waking up with a coffee from one of the many great local cafes, jumping in the water for a surf, refuelling with some exquisite local cuisine, and finishing the day off with just one of the many adventures this area has to offer. May it be fishing, hiking, more surfing, or beach walks at sunset, the end of most days here for us are magical ones.

Our love for surfing spills over into all aspects of the work we do. Whether you are an experienced surfer wanting to get to know our waters a bit better or have never dipped your toes in our Pacific waters, we promise to make your surf experience with us an unforgettable one.

We offer surf and stand-up paddle board lessons and rentals daily through all seasons. You will find us along Campbell St. across the street from **Storm Surf Shop** as you first enter town. Be sure to stop in, say hi, and get out in the water with us during your next visit to Tofino!

Hi! My name is **Thérèse Bouchard**. I first came to Tofino in the early eighties, to make it my home in '88. I have the privilege to work from my home, a beautiful glass studio with woodstove and inner garden, a creation from my beloved husband, Jan Janzen. This is where I have been practicing massage therapy for the last 28 years. I am a clinical hypno-therapist as well, and the director of clients services for Pacific Rim Hospice Society, for which I also do grief and loss support. With a different hat on, I teach African drumming.

I fell in love with Tofino during my first visit. I love the majestic intensity of the ocean, flora and fauna. I deeply appreciate the quietude that can be found in the surrounding nature, and the ease with which it can be accessed.

If I had only ONE day in Tofino, it would likely include a hike and picnic at Schooner Cove, and a meal at **SoBo restaurant.** Depending on the weather, I might add a paddle and a moonwalk.

I love this place. I feel blessed to call it home.

To book a session or buy a gift certificate, or to inquire about drumming lessons, please call 250-725-4278, or e-mail me at theresebouchard@yahoo.ca. I offer sessions from Thursday to Sunday, from 10:00 to 6:00. Winter hours (and days of work) are flexible.

My name is **Trina Mattson** and I have lived in Tofino for over 40 years... EEEK!

I love gardening, my dogs and my husband, not necessarily in that order.

I love that Tofino still has that feeling of small town, and when the chips are down we band together to help each other out.

I own and operate OCN Garden Center located at 619 Tibbs Plc about two miles out of town. We are open year round, so feel free to pop by and have a chat, you can also check out our FB page **OCN Garden Center**.

~~~~~~

Hi, my name is **Trish Dixon**. I grew up in Vancouver and moved to Tofino over 24 years ago. After many years of travel, my husband Tony and I opened Breakers Deli in 1997. Combining our love for travel and fresh local foods, we poured our heart and soul into Breakers for 14 years and loved every minute of it. I am a motivated member of the community, involving myself in many charities, event coordinating and volunteer work. I have been an active board member of the Surfrider Foundation for 15 years and have been involved in many community events.

Today you will find me at the beach, on a paddleboard, soaking up the sunshine or in the kitchen cooking up a storm for the multitude of family and friends I love to cook for. The bigger the dinner party the better!

In 2011, myself and a group of like-minded foodies, started Feast Tofino. **Feast Tofino** is a month long collaboration between acclaimed local and regional guest chefs, restaurants, fishermen, foragers and farmers, celebrating 'boat-to-table' cuisine. I presently am employed with the District of Tofino as an administrative assistant.

I love working with the community and learning how the municipality works from the public side. So many people work so hard to make this community such an amazing place to live.

I love Tofino for the natural beauty that surrounds us here and for the laid back lifestyle Tofino offers. Tofino offers our family the opportunity to live our life by harvesting foods that we either grow, hunt or forage on a year round basis. Many days you will find our teenage daughter Hana and her dad hunting or fishing, packing our freezers for the year with local wild seafood and venison. My inherited love for canning our own food keeps our pantry well stocked all year round. I challenge myself every year to can something that we would otherwise have bought from the grocery store. This not only replaces the plastic or tin packaging in our lives with glass, we now have foods that we grew or caught ourselves or purchased from local farmers. This year it was homemade relish and canning tuna. Today as I write this, I have made 24 jars of blackberry jam (blackberries from the **Long Beach Golf Course**- thanks, Gibby!).

Last year I had two of my best friends introduce me to a company called Life Vantage that has changed my life. The personal growth and desire to help so many live their best life, to be healthy, to spend time with our families and have the means to do so in a way that we all dream of. I am working on my future for my family with all the heart and passion for living that mirrors the life we have here in Tofino. We live a blessed life, and I am grateful daily.

~~~~~~~~~~~~~~~~~~~~~~~~~~~~~~~~~~~~~

Our names are **Victoria** Ashley and **Laurie,** and we are the owners of **Merge**, a store that conflates handmade goods with fine aesthetics. We have a passion for upcoming designs, creative people and we love supporting small entrepreneurs. We also strive to bring creativity to the community by hosting workshops in our little shop.

We love Tofino's young and vibrant people. We love our little but supportive community where no commercial chain businesses are allowed. And of course, we love the surroundings that allow us to live a healthy lifestyle, being able to enjoy the outdoors and the surf, which is really grounding.

Apart from owning and running a shop, we also are the designers behind our own brands. Victoria is the leatherworker behind Good Prospects as well as the idea girl offering branding consultations. Laurie is the artisan jeweller behind the hand-stamped jewelry line Highwaters as well as a freelance illustrator.

If we had ONE day in Tofino, we would go for a coffee at Tofino Coffee, have a morning walk to check out the surf beaches, treat ourselves to a **Red Can** breakfast and then go for a surf (or take a class if you are a beginner - very important!). For lunch time, we would hit **Tacofino** or **WildSide**. After, we would walk into town and check out the small businesses and of course Merge (behind the CIBC bank). Then, it's happy hour, and we would go to the brewery to enjoy a cold one. We would then have dinner at **Kuma** (because it's delicious!) and finish our long but awesome day in Tofino with some drinks at **Shelter** to get to feel the local vibe, friendly service and nice ambiance. That sounds like a perfect day but is actually a typical one in Tofino. That is why we think we are very lucky to be living here and hope you enjoy too!

Merge offers workshop throughout the year that you can check out on our website mergeartisancollective.com. We also offer customized items with our personal brands. Good Prospects can create custom pieces with a minimal aesthetic for any leather accessories that will fit your needs. Find more info check out her work on Instagram @goodprospects Highwaters can create a customize piece of jewelry with hand-stamped words on metal, directly from her workspace located in Merge, Tofino. It can be a souvenir from your trip in Tofino, words you live by or any other desire. You can find her jewelry work on **highwaters.me** and her illustration work on Instagram @laurieb.illustrations.

~~~~~~

Warren Rudd here, long time resident, cyclist, freelance news and documentary video guy.

I love Tofino because it's in Clayoquot Sound, which I love for its relative wildness, clean air and waters. It's not pristine anymore, but progress is being made and there are lots of areas that are still wild.

I shoot video for news of local stories, provide shots of major events that occurred here in the past (usually logging blockades) for documentaries from my archives, and produce videos for non-profits and First Nations locally and elsewhere in BC.

One day visiting in Tofino for me would include loading up on snacks and a smoothie or fresh juice for the day at Green Soul Organics, a Kayak or Paddleboard trip, a bike ride (rent if I didn't bring my own) along the Multi-Use Path and a ride or walk along Tonquin Park (Lighthouse trail) exploring all the lookouts. Then, if it was a Monday I would go to the movie at the **Clayoquot Sound Community Theatre** at Campbell and 2nd, making sure I arrive early (Doors at 7:15) so I had time to get a good seat (there's only 72!) and get a bowl of popcorn, a tea and a 'Movie Ball' at Warren's Organic Concession!

Unsung Heroes
(Keeping Tofino Safe behind the Scenes)

The unsung heroes of Tofino/ Clayoquot area are the people who work every day behind the scenes, sometimes out of the public eye, to ensure the safety of visitors and local residents. They are rarely mentioned, but they play a huge role in keeping the heart of Tofino alive.

Especially in summertime, I cannot stress enough the importance of these local women and men. With the daily population reaching 20,000 at times, they maintain the infrastructure, security, and safety of the community. Minimizing theft, disorderly conduct, littering, and environmental disrespect are examples of the wonderful things they do.

Bylaw Officers

Our bylaw officers are the enforcers of our community's bylaws, which in turn promote community livability by maintaining the health, safety and general wellness of our community. Without them, there would be much disorganized chaos. They ultimately assist in maintaining community standards such as traffic bylaws, animal control, illegal camping, illegal beach fires, and noise complaints. They regularly patrol local beaches within the municipality and the town of Tofino.

Municipal Office
250-725-4435
bylaw@tofino.ca

Parks Canada Wardens

In our national park and marine conservation areas, the parks wardens have very important roles. Their main duties are to protect natural and cultural resources, patrol park's campgrounds, and ensure the safety of visitors. They are considered "peace officers" and are allowed to carry firearms.

250-726-3500
www.pacrim.info@pc.gc.ca

RCMP

In Canada, a Royal Canadian Mounted Police Officer, also known as a Mounty, is a national symbol. In Tofino and surrounding areas, we have the Royal Canadian Mounted Police Officers who provide front-line policing, municipally and provincially. Our Tofino RCMP detachment serves not only Tofino, but the neighboring communities of Opitsaht, Ahousaht, Hesquiaht, Pacific Rim National Park, and elsewhere in Clayoquot Sound. My hat definitely goes off to them.

Contact Note

The dispatch center is located in Courtney, and they look after the entire North Island and are very familiar with Tofino. The Tofino RCMP office is not always manned, so you need to simply use the phone outside for non-emergencies (emergencies dial 9-1-1) to call the dispatch center by following prompts.

RCMP Detachment Contact

Emergency	**9-1-1**
Detachment Office	250-725-3242 (non-emergency)

Location
400 Campbell St, Tofino across from the Municipal Office.

The Local Nuu-chah-nulth Nations
The local Nuu-chah-nulth are composed of two main local communities: the Ahousaht First Nation and the Tla-o-qui-aht First Nation. Traditionally for thousands of years and unofficially to this day, the people of these communities have been and are still the guardians of our coast. The watermen of these coastal communities know these waters like the back of their hand and are usually the first to respond and help in marine situations.

Volunteer Firefighters
Our Tofino Volunteer Fire Department are, that's right, all volunteers! They do not get paid to save lives and be the first on the scene of an accident. Our fire fighters are dedicated and committed people who do what they do because they love helping people, and we love them for it! Their mission is to provide a quality fire/ rescue service to our community and its visitors.

Fire Department Contact

Emergency	**9-1-1**
Fire Department Office	250-725-3365 (non-emergency)

Fire Department Officers

Fire Chief	John Gilmour
Captain	Donny Collins
Captain	Billy McGinnis

Fire Department Personnel

• Chief • Officers, 2 volunteers • Fire Fighters, 18 volunteers

Location

The Tofino Fire Hall is located in Centre of Tofino at 150 Second Street.

All of the fire department info was taken from this site: http://tofino.ca/ content/tofino-volunteer-fire-department

Canadian Coast Guard

Canadian Coast Guard services support government priorities and economic prosperity and contribute to the safety, accessibility and security of Canadian waters. They are a government marine organization with no naval or law enforcement responsibilities.

Canadian Coast Guard Station Tofino Contact

Emergency VHF Radio	Channel 16
Coast Guard Office	250-725-3231

Location

326 Main Street, Tofino

Westcoast Inland Search & Rescue

WISAR, a non-profit organization, was formed by dedicated volunteers who are in the process of developing a local search and rescue capability for the Clayoquot Region. They depend on donations and fundraising activities to support their operations.

To make a donation visit www.westcoastsar.org

Tofino Dentist

Bad toothache? Need emergency dental work? Dr. James Jameson is our Tofino dentist and can help.

311 Neill St. below SoBo Restaurant
250-725-2068

Long Beach Automotive

Car trouble? Do not despair! Long Beach Automotive is our locally owned, family operated mechanic shop who are here to help with any car problems you may encounter during your trip. Owners Dave and Sarah are wonderful.

Unit #3, 671 Industrial Way (up the hill from Tofino Brew Co.)
250-725-2030

Roadside Assistance 24/7: 1-866-345-9060 (includes CAA/AAA)
www.longbeachauto.ca

Tofino/Ucluelet Ambulance Service

Ambulance Paramedic Contact

Emergency	9-1-1
Tofino Ambulance Service	250-725-2252 (non-emergency)

Tonquin Medical Clinic & Tofino Hospital Staff

All of our wonderful local Tofino hospital staff as well as our Tonquin Medical Clinic staff including the doctors, nurses, and technicians are Tofino's health care providers. They help anyone in the community when they are sick or in medical emergency. They always have their hands full once the summer season rolls around.

Tofino General Hospital Contact

Emergency	**9-1-1**
Reception	250-725-4010

Location: 261 Neill Street, Tofino

Tonquin Medical Clinic Contact

Emergency	**9-1-1**
Reception	250-725-3282

Location: 220 First Street, Tofino

British Columbia Conservation Officer Service

Conservation Officers in the Tofino area are responsible for protecting the environment and the natural resources of the designated area. Like the park wardens, they are considered peace officers and are allowed to carry firearms.

They are public safety providers focused on natural resource law enforcement and human wildlife conflicts prevention and response.

To report a conflict with wildlife that threatens public safety, or the safety of the animal, call 1-877-952-7277

Small Business = Giant Impact

Kait's 13 REASONS Why Everyone Should Buy Local/ Support Local Business:

01   **MONEY stays within the local economy**, thereby enriching the local community. Cloned box chain stores suck a very high percentage of the revenue out of the local economy and destroy a town's character.

02   **Builds LOCAL CHARACTER and prosperity.** Communities that protect and preserve their unique small businesses develop an economic advantage.

03   **More JOBS are created locally.** Wages and benefits in most sectors are better versus chain stores.

04   **Instills and STRENGTHENS COMMUNITY!** Locally owned business is the backbone to a strong community. Lively town centers are created, boosting the arts and a vibrant culture interlinking neighbors and creating a supportive social center that upholds local causes.

05   Promotes **LOCAL DECISION-MAKING.**
Businesses being owned and operated by locals ensures
that important decisions are made locally by the people
who reside there and who will be impacted by those
decisions thereby dodging many unforeseen problems
that can be created when decisions are made outside.

06   **ENTREPRENEURSHIP!** I personally believe Tofino
has one of the best environments for entrepreneurs in
Canada. Why? Local businesses are protected. Without
entrepreneurship, there's no innovation, no prosperity;
entrepreneurship serves as the key means for families to
move up the economic ladder.

07   **Creates COMPETITION.** A community where there
are various small businesses is the best way to insure
innovation and low prices long term.

08   **SOCIAL RESPONSIBILITY.** Items are normally
sourced more responsibly and locally, versus the
exploitation of international human resources. As well,
products are usually better quality.

09   **Product DIVERSITY.** Ever notice that all box chain
stores carry roughly the same product? Products aren't
selected based on a national sales plan here; they are
selected to satisfy the local needs, and this guarantees
a much broader range of products. If we want/need
something at our local Coop Grocery, or Beaches
Grocery, we ask, and if there's a strong enough local
demand, we get it.

10 **Environmental SUSTAINABILITY/ RESPONSIBILITY!** Small businesses have normally a lower footprint and greater respect for their surroundings because we live here! As well, many larger corporate structures, especially restaurants, have more one-use items thereby creating more trash to dispose of.

11 **Better COMMUNICATION!** Small businesses know their customers better.

12 **The people PAY LESS.** Tax payers generally pay more to provide big-boxed stores with services such as road maintenance, fire, police, etc. Also, big public subsidies that finance the expansion of big-box chain stores fail to generate real economic benefits.

13 **CHARITABLE CONTRIBUTIONS**, the act of giving. According to studies, small businesses donate roughly TWICE as much per employee compared to large businesses.

Need I go any further? All of these benefits affect every single person, indirectly or directly. How can we protect small businesses? SHOP AND BUY LOCAL. Take a stand for local business; in the end your community will thank you. THANK YOU!

Closing Words

Tofino isn't just the "End of the Road", but the beginning of a new road. I hope everyone who witnesses the beauty of Clayoquot will walk away feeling kissed by Mother Nature herself and will bring back a renewed greater appreciation, respect for the wild, the natural world, and a deeper understanding for why the First Peoples protected and took very good care of this land and water for many thousands of years.

Stepping into an old growth temperate rainforest is a very magical experience. All of a sudden, the world becomes mute, peaceful, serene, and time slows. You become enveloped in multiple shades of green, yellow and brown. You become protected from the elements. No wind, no rain can touch you. Even though it's quiet as a mouse, there is so much life around you. It connects you with what's important in life.

As Tofitians, we learn to coexist with nature, with our environment. Wasps may be annoying, but hey with them they bring warm sunny weather (one reason to appreciate the wet, rainy days...no wasps!) and wasps, believe it or not, have tons of benefits to our ecosystem.

We love to reuse, recycle, compost and protect the environment! Open the cupboards of many Tofitian homes and you'll usually find glass mason jars and recycled glass jars as glassware. Maybe you can find some neat ways to reuse items during your stay, be creative.

The support system to any community is dining local, eating local, shopping local. We all work together and we all just happen to love Tofino and Canadian made goods!

Busy summer times combined with limited housing, can create a staff shortage for many local businesses. We have limited space because we want to keep our wild, but we want more space for you to come and visit! Staff shortages are very common, and when a business fails to reach your expectations, please give them a second chance.

Keep the wild in wild. Give wildlife their space, especially bears, wolves, and whales, and this will keep them around for many more years to come.

We love the rain, otherwise we would never live here. What's a rainforest without rain? Jump into those rain boots, throw on a good rain jacket and rain pants and enjoy the many things we have around us that wouldn't be there without rain! Last minute challenge: try to build a beach fire in the rain.

Now you are officially a well-informed Tofitian to be! Get out, explore, relax, learn, ask questions, and don't be afraid to get your hands dirty...or wet! I've shown you MY Tofino, What's YOURS?

About the Author

At 28, Kait Fennell can list off more accomplishments than some people twice her age, including entrepreneur, commercial pilot, world traveler and now first time author. She is also a competitive surfer and has trained with some of the top female surfers in the international surfing world.

A National Scholar through the Garfield Weston Scholarship Foundation, Kait studied hard and earned her BA degree in Applied Tech and Commercial Pilot License from Seneca College. She remained in Toronto for an additional year to develop a special, green energy aircraft designed to fly in needed medical and other supplies to the most remote areas of Africa as well as bringing in supplies to remote areas of Canada.

In addition to being an avid aviator and surfer, Kait has also shown a scholarly side from an early age. Her first brush with publication came during her last year of high school. Her essay "Should the Bras D'Or Lake and its Watershed Become a United Nations World Biosphere Reserve" was not only published but sparked real talk as well- with that very thing happening a mere five years later.

Want to know what 251 Things To Do is up to?
Subscribe to our website: *www.251thingstodo.com*

47395202R00114

Made in the USA
Lexington, KY
08 August 2019